CHAMPIONS OF FREEDOM

The Ludwig von Mises Lecture Series

CHAMPIONS OF FREEDOM

Volume 24

THE FUTURE OF AMERICAN BUSINESS

Richard M. Ebeling, Executive Editor

Lissa Roche, General Editor

Hillsdale College Press
Hillsdale, Michigan 49242

Hillsdale College Press

Books by the Hillsdale College Press include The Christian Vision series; Champions of Freedom series; and other works.

The views expressed in this volume are not necessarily the views of Hillsdale College.

The Champions of Freedom series
THE FUTURE OF AMERICAN BUSINESS
©1996 Hillsdale College Press, Hillsdale, Michigan 49242

Printed in the United States of America

Photo: New York Commodities Exchange, Gold
©1996 Eric Kroll/Omni-Photo Communications

First printing 1996

Library of Congress Catalog Card Number 96-076994
ISBN 0-916308-64-2

Contents

RECOMMENDED READING

Contributors

RICHARD M. EBELING is the Ludwig von Mises Professor of Economics at Hillsdale College. A former professor at the University of Dallas, he joined the Hillsdale faculty in 1988. In addition, he serves on the editorial board of the *Review of Austrian Economics* and as vice president of the Future of Freedom Foundation. He has edited *Money, Method, and the Market Process: Essays by Ludwig von Mises* and a number of volumes in the Hillsdale College Press Champions of Freedom series; he is also co-editor of *The Dangers of Socialized Medicine.*

Professor Ebeling has lectured extensively on privatization and monetary reform throughout the United States, Latin America, and the former Soviet Union, where he has consulted with the Lithuanian government, the city of Moscow, and the Russian parliament.

JOHN ENGLER was elected the 46th governor of Michigan in 1990. He immediately launched the "Taxpayers' Agenda," a bold strategy to cut taxes, downsize government, create jobs, and improve Michigan's business climate and public education. He was reelected in 1994 with 62 percent of the vote—

the largest victory for a Republican governor since 1928 and the second largest for any governor in Michigan history. He has signed more than 100 anti-crime bills, dramatically cut property taxes, reformed state welfare programs, and won approval for one of the nation's most ambitious charter school experiments.

Governor Engler holds degrees from Michigan State University and the Thomas M. Cooley School of Law. He served for eight years in the Michigan House of Representatives and twelve years in the Michigan Senate, where he was majority leader from 1983 to 1990. He and his wife, Michelle, are the proud parents of triplets.

As chairman and chief executive officer, CHARLES KOCH has presided over the dramatic growth of Koch Industries. Under his leadership, this energy-based firm has grown from $177 million in sales in 1966 to over $20 billion today, and it ranks as the second largest privately held company in America and one of the largest in the world.

Mr. Koch is dedicated to developing Market-Based Management,® an approach that draws insight from the productivity of the free marketplace. He has helped establish centers to study Market-Based Management® at the University of Kansas and George Mason University. His commitment also carries over to his philanthropic interests, which include funding programs that apply market solutions to social problems. He was instrumental in founding the Cato Institute and Citizens for a Sound Economy. He serves as chairman of the board of the Institute for Humane Studies and the Center for Market Processes.

PHILLIP J. MEDDINGS is the founder and chairman in Australia and the United Kingdom of The Executive Committee (TEC), a company designed to bring together chief executives into regular group meetings with the object of increasing their effectiveness as leaders and managers through continuing business education.

He was formerly the chief executive officer of a large Australasian conglomerate, Mauri Brothers & Thomson, where he created and implemented a plan to expand into a global business focused on fermentation products. Today, the conglomerate is the largest baker's yeast and vinegar company in the world.

Dr. Meddings holds a Ph.D. in chemical engineering from Monash University in Australia. He currently resides in London.

VICTOR NIEDERHOFFER is a speculator. He received his Ph.D. from the University of Chicago Business School in 1969, and he taught at the University of California-Berkeley for five years. He has published widely on the scientific aspects of markets.

Mr. Niederhoffer also owns a variety of businesses. In the 1980s, he was one of the nation's top pro racquetball players and he has won numerous championships in squash and paddleball.

LAWRENCE W. REED is president of the Mackinac Center for Public Policy, a Michigan-based think tank dedicated to market-oriented education and research; he is a past president of the State Policy Network, a national organization of 40 regional policy groups. He holds an M.A. degree in history from Slippery Rock State University, and he is the former chairman of the department of economics at Northwood University. In the past 10 years, he has authored over 600 newspaper columns, 300 radio commentaries, dozens of magazine articles, and four books, the most recent of which is *Lessons from the Past: The Silver Panic of 1893*.

Mr. Reed's interests in political and economic affairs have taken him to 55 countries on six continents. While traveling with members of the Polish anti-communist underground some years ago, he was arrested and detained. Also from firsthand experience, he has reported on hyperinflation in South America, voodoo in Haiti, black markets in Russia, and rebel warfare in the bush in Nicaragua and Mozambique.

ANDREA MILLEN RICH began her career at the CBS television network. After stints at the Leo Burnett Advertising Agency and Jaffe Productions, where she edited *The Joe Pyne Show* for both radio and TV syndication, and her own production company, she worked as a writer/researcher in the NBC-TV elections unit from 1972 to 1974. She also owned and operated a used paperback bookstore in upstate New York.

In 1982, she became president and owner of Laissez Faire Books, which distributes "the world's largest selection of books on liberty," and keeps in print many free market classics such as *Human Action, The Discovery of Freedom,* and *Economics in One Lesson.* In 1994, *Forbes* magazine profiled Mrs. Rich as one of America's leading American businesswomen.

GEORGE ROCHE has served as president of Hillsdale College since 1971. Formerly the presidentially appointed chairman of the National Council on Education Research, the director of seminars at the Foundation for Economic Education, a professor of history at the Colorado School of Mines, and a U.S. Marine, he is the author of twelve books, including six Conservative Book Club selections.

His latest book is *The Fall of the Ivory Tower: Government Funding, Corruption, and the Bankrupting of American Higher Education.* Reviews and excerpts have appeared in many sources, including *Forbes,* the *Wall Street Journal,* and *Reader's Digest.* It was also the subject of a cover story in the spring 1994 issue of *Insight* magazine; the editors named it the "Book of the Year." *Los Angeles Times* syndicated columnist Cal Thomas has called it "The most important book on higher education since *The Closing of the American Mind.*"

HARRY E. TEASLEY, JR., is a recently retired, 35-year veteran of the Coca-Cola Company, where he served in a variety of leadership positions, including vice president, Coca-Cola US; vice president of corporate business development, the Coca-Cola

Company; president and CEO of the Wine Spectrum; managing director of Coca-Cola's bottling operations in the UK; president and CEO of Coca-Cola Foods; and president and CEO of the Coca-Cola Nestle Refreshments Company.

Mr. Teasley also serves as a trustee on a number of boards, including Georgia Tech Foundation; the Georgia Tech School of Industrial Engineering; the University of Tampa; SunBank of Tampa Bay; the Tampa Bay Performing Arts Center; and the Reason Foundation, where he serves as chairman.

DAVE THOMAS started in the restaurant business as a busboy at age 15. Shortly before turning 18, he joined the U.S. Army, where he gained additional experience in his chosen field. After his military service ended, he became a short-order cook. Soon, he realized his dream, opening his own restaurant with a partner. In 1962, he took on a new challenge: turning around four failing Kentucky Fried Chicken restaurants. He did so, and six years later became a millionaire at age 35.

Mr. Thomas opened the first Wendy's Old Fashioned Hamburgers restaurant in 1969 and established the Wendy's franchise in 1973. Instead of selling single franchises, he pioneered the practice of selling franchises for entire cities and regions. Today, there are more than 5,000 Wendy's worldwide. Mr. Thomas is known for his famous commercial appearances; he is also a noted philanthropist, working with many children's hospitals, medical research institutes, and private charities. In 1992, he established the Dave Thomas Foundation for Adoption, which is supported by the sales of his books, *Dave's Way* and *Well Done!*

One of the nation's leading experts on the privatization of government services, CHARLES D. VAN EATON holds the Evert McCabe/UPS Chair in economics at Hillsdale College where he has been department chairman for the past seventeen years. As chair, he has helped develop an economics curriculum unique among undergraduate institutions in its emphasis on the work of two of the world's most important economists, F. A. Hayek and Ludwig von Mises.

He has been the principal author of a number of widely remarked studies, including "Revitalizing the American City: A Market Perspective for Detroit"; "Privatization: Theory and Practice for Michigan"; "Jail Overcrowding: A Public Problem with a Private Solution?"; and "Managing the Michigan Solid Waste Stream: Markets or Mandates?" He has also testified frequently before state legislatures, county and municipal organizations and engineering societies, and served as a privatization consultant for cities and school districts.

In addition to his Ph.D. in economics from Tulane University, Dr. Van Eaton was trained in theology at both Freed-Hardeman University in Tennessee and Harding University in Arkansas. He is an ordained minister in the Churches of Christ.

Foreword

For seventeen years, America's most distinguished scholars and active decisionmakers have met on the Hillsdale College campus to pay homage to one of the world's greatest champions of freedom, Austrian School economist Ludwig von Mises (1881-1973). Perhaps the College's proudest possession is Mises's personal library. Upon bequeathing his library to us, Professor Mises said he had done so because "Hillsdale, more than any other educational institution, most strongly represents the free market ideas to which I have given my life."

When the history of the 20th century is written, the Mises name will surely be remembered as that of the foremost economist of our age. Certainly the history of one period during this century ought to include his name writ large: the one in which we are now living, the one that will be forever remembered as the time when the Berlin Wall finally came crashing down. The man who took out the first brick was Ludwig von Mises. He did it with books such as *The Theory of Money and Credit, The Free and Prosperous Commonwealth, Omnipotent Government, Bureaucracy,* and *Human Action.*

Mises based his theory of economics on the supremacy of the individual. The rational, purposeful, day-to-day decisions of ordinary men and women are what constitute the market and are the basis of all human action. It was his understanding of the market as a process, against the background of continually changing conditions and limited individual knowledge, that set his theory so clearly apart from the rigid, mathematical attempts of other economists bent on devising "models" of equilibrium.

Few economists perceived so clearly the consequences of the ideas set in motion by the statist and collectivist mentality. He warned that the greatest danger to Western society would come with the increasing concentration of political and economic power in the hands of the state. He used the example of communism in the Soviet Union and Eastern Europe to point out that the peril was real indeed.

It was Mises who wrote so eloquently and forcefully that the state could never successfully control the marketplace any more than it could control the lives of men. In fact, Mises's testimony finally convinced prominent Marxist–Leninist intellectuals to admit in the 1980s, "The world is run by human action, not by human design."

This 24th volume of the Champions of Freedom series is based on the same premise, and it explores the future of American business in the context of Mises's important and enduring intellectual legacy.

September 1996   GEORGE ROCHE
                                        President
                                        Hillsdale College

Introduction

In 1886, Walter R. Houghton, professor of political science at Indiana University, published a 620-page book titled *Kings of Fortune, or The Triumphs and Achievements of Noble, Self-Made Men.* Professor Houghton referred to these individuals as men "Whose brilliant careers have honored their calling, blessed humanity, and whose lives furnish instruction for the young, entertainment for the old, and valuable lessons for the aspirants of fortune." And in the preface, he added, "The chief glory of America is that it is the country in which genius and industry find their speediest and surest reward. Fame and fortune are here open to all who are willing to work for them. Neither class distinction nor social prejudices, neither differences of birth, religion, nor ideas, can prevent the man of true merit from winning the just reward of his labors in this favored land. We are emphatically a nation of self-made men, and it is to the labors of this worthy class that our marvelous national prosperity is due."[1]

Professor Houghton went out of his way to emphasize that genius and fame was not defined by him merely in monetary terms. He was recounting the stories also of men who did not always amass great wealth but who had made lasting contributions in their chosen vocation. However, he clearly did not think these people somehow more noble or worthy of attention merely because they had not accumulated monetary

1

riches. In his histories of the lives of "noble, self-made men," wealth was nothing to be ashamed of. Instead, accumulated wealth was the mark of a man who had applied his intellectual capabilities and, through honest, dedicated, and disciplined effort, had made his fortune by revolutionizing the manufacturing or marketing of the goods and services available to the masses of the American people in the free marketplace.

The United States was the first country founded on the principle of commerce, trade, and the primacy of peaceful, voluntary exchange. In the 1830s, a French traveler named Michel Chevalier spent two years exploring American life. He returned to France and published a book recounting his journey. The volume appeared in an English translation in 1839. "It must be allowed that [the] ardent and entire devotion to business [in America] gives the nation a strange aspect in the eyes of a European," Chevalier said. "But the more interesting consideration is, whether the Americans of our day do not fulfill, as perfectly as human nature is capable of doing, the mission which Providence has entrusted to them, that of acting as a nation of pioneers and subduers of the forest." He went on:

> The American is a model of industry. This country ... is a gigantic commercial house, which owns its wheat-fields in the Northwest, its cotton, rice and tobacco plantations in the South, which maintains its sugar works, its establishments for salting provisions, and some good beginnings of manufactures, which has its harbors in the Northeast thronged with fine ships, well built and better manned, by means of which it undertakes to carry for the world, and to speculate on the wants of all nations. . . .
>
> Figure to yourself an Irish peasant who at home could scarcely earn enough to live on potatoes, who would look upon himself as a rich man if he owned an acre of ground, but who, upon stepping ashore at New York, finds himself able to earn a dollar a day by the mere strength of

his arm. He feeds and lodges himself for two dollars a week, and at the end of a fortnight he may have saved enough to buy ten acres of the most fertile land in the world. The distance from New York to the West is great, it is true, but the fare on the great canal is trifling, and he can easily pay his way by work of his hands. It is also true, that the poorest Irishman would not think of buying so little as ten acres; the least that one buys in the West is eighty....

The manners and customs are altogether those of a working, busy society. At the age of 15 years, a man is engaged in business; at twenty-one he is established, he has his farm, work-shop, his counting house, or his office, in a word his employment, whatever it may be. He now also takes a wife, and at twenty-two is the father of a family, and consequently has a powerful stimulus to excite his industry. A man who has no profession, and, which is the nearly same thing, who is not married, enjoys little consideration; he, who is an active and useful member of society, who contributes his share to augment the national wealth and increase the numbers of the population, he only is looked upon with respect and favor. The American is educated with the idea that he will have some particular occupation, that he is to be a farmer, artisan, manufacturer, merchant, speculator, lawyer, physician, or minister, perhaps all in succession, and that, if he is active and intelligent, he will make his fortune. He has no conception of living without a profession, even when his family is rich, for he sees nobody about him not engaged in business. The man of leisure is a variety of the human species of which the Yankee does not suspect the existence, and he knows that if rich today, his father may be ruined tomorrow. Besides the father himself is engaged in business according to custom, and does not think of dispossessing himself of his fortune; if his son wishes to have one at present, let him make it himself....

> Unlimited competition [is] the sole law of labor, everyone
> being his own master.... An American's business is al-
> ways to be on the edge lest his neighbor get there before
> him. If a hundred Americans were about to go before
> the firing squad, they would start fighting for the priv-
> ilege to go first, so used are they to competition.[2]

Humor aside, this is the spirit that made America great. And
the government, at all levels—whether it be federal, state, or
local—kept practically completely out of the way. Government's
primary function was to protect the life, liberty, and property of the individual. Did the government sometimes inter-
fere in the marketplace and busy itself with scandalous wastes
of money on public works, or subsidies on enterprises run
by men close to those who controlled the public purse? Yes,
it did.[3] But these were invariably considered evil examples
of political corruption and almost always economic disasters.[4]
The hallmark of the American system was freedom of enterprise and an open road for the risk-taking speculator and
entrepreneur.

In the 20th century, under the influence of socialist and
interventionist-welfare statist ideas, American business and
the creative entrepreneur have come under increasing regulation and control by the government. Just how regulated
are the U.S. economy and the American businessman? Here
is a *partial* list of the federal agencies that have regulatory
or some form of interventionist authority over the various
sectors and activities of the American marketplace: the Office of Science and Technology Policy; Commission on Civil
Rights; Commodity Futures Trading Commission; Consumer
Protection Agency; Environmental Protection Agency; Equal
Opportunity Commission; Export-Import Bank; Farm Credit Administration; Federal Communications Commission; Federal Deposit Insurance Corporation; Federal Housing Finance
Board; Federal Labor Relations Authority; Federal Mine Safety
and Health Review Commission; Federal Reserve System; Federal Trade Commission; Interstate Commerce Commission;

National Aeronautics and Space Administration; National Foundation of the Arts and the Humanities; National Labor Relations Board; National Railroad Passenger Corporation (Amtrak); National Science Foundation; National Transportation Safety Board; Nuclear Regulatory Commission; Occupational Safety and Health Review Commission; Resolution Trust Commission; Securities and Exchange Commission; Small Business Administration; Tennessee Valley Authority; Thrift Depositor Protection Oversight Board; Trade and Development Agency; United States International Trade Commission; United States Postal Service; Bureau of Alcohol, Tobacco and Firearms; Bureau of Indian Affairs; Federal Aviation Administration; Federal Highway Administration; Fish and Wildlife Service; Food and Drug Administration; Forest Service; Immigration and Naturalization Service; Internal Revenue Service; National Institutes of Health; National Oceanic and Atmospheric Administration; National Park Service; Social Security Administration; and the Surgeon General's Office.

Can anyone look at this list of government agencies and say with a straight face that the American enterprise system is still "free"? It would be a far more difficult task to find those corners of the U.S. economy that are not *unfree!* And added to the labyrinth of regulations and controls is, of course, the tax burden on every facet of enterprise in America.

The question that now faces the United States is what path will it follow during the century that lies just ahead? Will we continue down the path of greater and greater government control over the market and the entrepreneur? Or will we return to the political–economic foundations upon which this nation of ours was born? Will some visitor from some other part of the world travel around America in the 2030s, the way Michel Chevalier did in the 1830s, and see an America that is free, industrious, and innovative, with the greatest latitude given to the creative enterpriser? Or will he see an America straightjacketed in regulations and controls, weighed down with burdensome taxes, with corrupted and corrupting welfare-redistributionist programs, and businessmen who devote more of their time to the political games of high-stakes lobbying and intrigue to survive than to the normal and healthy business of making better and less expensive products to improve the lives of consumers?

Austrian School economist Ludwig von Mises, in whose name these essays are dedicated, was a champion of the free market economy. In his numerous writings, he devoted his life to defending individual freedom and unhampered markets; he emphasized with a greater clarity than many others that it is the entrepreneur who is the prime mover of material progress. As he argued, "The driving force of the market process is provided neither by the consumers nor by the owners of the means of production—land, capital goods, and labor—but by the promoting and speculating entrepreneurs."[5]

Consumers do not themselves directly call goods into existence; owners of the means of production do not automatically combine themselves for the achievement of various productive activities. There must be individuals who imagine possibilities for the future, guided by what they conceive as possible consumer wants of tomorrow; these same individuals must imagine ways and means of combining those factors of production in a manner that can turn the raw materials of the world into useful products. In competition with each other, the enterprising entrepreneurs bid for the purchase or hire of the means of production and then, when their respective processes of production are done, offer their wares to the buying public.

It is at that point that it is discovered whether the entrepreneurs have correctly anticipated better than their rivals what consumers may actually be willing to buy and whether, in fact, they have been able to manufacture those goods with the desired qualities and characteristics—at prices more attractive than what their competitors are offering. If they have succeeded in this endeavor, they earn profits; if not, they may be faced with losses. The process of profit and loss constantly and continuously changes the ownership over productive property and wealth, from less entrepreneurially competent hands to those who are more competent—both in devising evernewer and better methods of production and in demonstrating the greater ability in reading the signs as to where markets will be moving in the future.

But this dynamic and creative competitive process cannot function effectively or efficiently if burdened with a spider's web of regulations, controls, and taxes. Freedom is the prerequisite for prosperity. It is what America will need a lot more of if it is to flourish in the century ahead. The speakers at the 1996 Ludwig von Mises Lecture series at Hillsdale College addressed themselves to various aspects of this challenge. Together they offer a vision and a hope for the future of American business.

RICHARD M. EBELING
Ludwig von Mises Professor
of Economics
Hillsdale College

Notes

[1] Walter R. Houghton, *Kings of Fortune, or The Triumphs and Achievements of Noble, Self-Made Men* (Chicago: A. E. Davis & Co., 1886), 5-6.

[2] All quotes from Michel Chevalier's book are taken from William E. Rappard, *The Secret of American Prosperity* (New York: Greenberg Publishers, 1955), 53-59.

[3] See Jonathan R. T. Hughes, *The Governmental Habit Redux: Economic Controls from Colonial Times to the Present* (Princeton, NJ: Princeton University Press, 1991).

[4] See Warren M. Persons, *Government Experimentation in Business* (New York: John Wiley & Sons, Inc., 1934).

[5] Ludwig von Mises, *Human Action, A Treatise on Economics*, 3rd ed. rev. (Chicago: Henry Regnery Co., 1966), 328.

RICHARD M. EBELING

The Global Economy and Classical Liberalism: Past, Present, and Future

The United States in the Global Economy

Reading the headlines of the daily newspapers or watching the evening television news, the world seems like a extremely dangerous place. If a visitor from another planet were to try to draw conclusions about what human existence on earth is all about just from looking at the popular news sources, he would easily have the impression that our world is filled with nothing but wars, civil wars, ethnic conflicts, terrorist acts, organized criminal activity, and random violence.

Unfortunately, these things are occurring in many places around the world and they create a degree of suffering, hardship, destruction, and cruelty that is often beyond the human imagination to fully comprehend. Many people do live in social environments that truly represent a human existence that is often "nasty, brutish, and short."

But there is another world, one that does not fill the newspaper headlines every day and which is not as frequently depicted in the flickering pictures that cross our television screens. This is the world of commerce, industry, and international exchange. For probably almost half the population of the world, and especially in Western Europe, North and

9

South America, Australia, and increasing portions of Asia and Eastern Europe, life is relatively peaceful and orderly. Production, not plunder, envelops the affairs of daily life. Precisely because of its common and mundane routine, it does not receive the same attention as do violent acts. The world has a lot of peace and prosperity. It just goes unnoticed unless we stop and think about what we take for granted around us. This is the world of everyday life that the United States participates in and with which it is increasingly interdependent.

Perhaps some numbers will make this more obvious:

- In spite of passport requirements and visa restrictions, 45.4 million people visited the United States in 1994; they spent almost $78 billion during their travels in this country. Significantly, while the total number of visitors to the U.S. was about the same as the previous year, foreign tourist spending was more than 4.5 percent greater.

- In 1994, direct U.S. investment around the world totaled over $612 billion. Nearly half was invested in Europe and about one-sixth was invested in the Asia–Pacific region, including Japan.

- In the same year, direct foreign investment in the U.S. totaled over $504 billion. More than half of this sum was invested by Europeans and only a little over one-fifth was invested by Asians, including the Japanese.

- Between 1993 and 1994, U.S. direct investment around the world increased by over 9.2 percent, while foreign direct investment in the U.S. rose by about 8.6 percent. During this period, direct U.S. investment in Europe rose by 7 percent and in the Asia–Pacific region rose by more than 17 percent.

- During those years, the Japanese only increased their direct investment in the U.S. by about 4 percent. The Swiss increased theirs by 14 percent; the French, 13.9 percent; the Germans, 13.8 percent; and the British, 10.9 percent.

•In 1994, the United States exported almost $840 billion in goods, services, and income, while importing almost $955 billion. Of our total exports, only about $45 billion was in the form of agricultural products, while over $402 billion was in manufactured goods.

•Between 1993 and 1994, U.S. exports rose over 11 percent and our imports rose almost 15.5 percent. (U.S. agricultural exports increased about 7 percent, while U.S. manufacturing exports rose more than 10 percent.) In 1994, U.S. exports represented close to 15.4 percent of the Gross National Product (GNP).[1]

The United States and many other nations have truly become an increasingly interdependent global economy, one in which goods move across borders far more often than do armies.

The Sesquicentennial of the Triumph of Free Trade

In appreciating the fact that the world has become an increasingly global marketplace, it is worth keeping in mind that this is a relatively new phenomenon in modern human history. Two hundred years ago, the dominant nation-states of Europe were imbued with the ideology of mercantilism, the 18th century's version of the regulated and planned economy.[2] The mercantilist system began to be systematically challenged only in the middle of the 18th century. The challenge was mounted on the European continent by the French Physiocrats and in England by the Scottish moral philosophers led by David Hume and Adam Smith. Adam Smith's *The Wealth of Nations* has justly come to be considered one of the intellectual fountainheads of modern economic liberty. With a brilliant combination of logic and historical example, Smith demonstrated, as few others had up to his day, that governmental controls, regulations, and restrictions on economic freedom were the fundamental causes of extensive poverty, misuse of resources, and pervasive political corruption. He declared that what England—and, indeed, any country—needed if it desired increased prosperity for all, wise use of its resources, and greater justice in human relationships was a "system of natural liberty." Under such a system, Smith argued, "Every man, as long as he does not violate the laws of justice, is left perfectly free to pursue his own interest his own way, and to bring both his industry and capital into competition with those of any other man, or order of men.... The sovereign is completely discharged from a duty... of which no human wisdom or knowledge could ever be sufficient; the duty of superintending the industry of private people, and of directing it towards employments most suitable to the interest of society."[3]

The government, in Smith's view, would be limited to three functions: (1) protection of the citizenry from foreign aggression; (2) the protection of the citizenry from domestic robbery and murder, which meant establishing a judicial system to administer justice; and, (3) the provision of a number of limited public works that Smith believed might not be profitable for private citizens to provide but which might have a wider usefulness for the society.

But in spite of the eloquence and rigor with which Smith demonstrated the harm and futility of the mercantilist forms of planning and regulation in his day, he despaired that economic freedom would ever be triumphant. "To expect, indeed, that the freedom of trade should ever be entirely restored to Great Britain," he said, "is as absurd as to expect that an Oceana or Utopia should ever be established in it. Not only the prejudices of the public, but what is much more unconquerable, the private interests of many individuals irresistibly oppose it."[4]

And, in fact, the next several decades following Adam Smith's death in 1790 seemed to bear out his pessimism. While under the prime ministership of William Pitt in the 1780s, Great Britain moved in directions more in line with the types of trade policies advocated by Smith. These directions reversed in the

1790s after the start of the wars that Britain began to fight with first revolutionary and then Napoleonic France. New protectionist trade barriers were imposed in the name of the war effort. Britain and France both tried to enforce naval blockades against each other. Only a pervasive network of smuggling throughout Europe prevented many from going without food or clothing.[5] As Francis Hirst explained in his book, *From Adam Smith to Philip Snowden: A History of Free Trade*, "When peace came in 1815 it found Great Britain exhausted by 22 years of war and Protection."[6]

But instead of reversing the controls and regulations, the British Parliament passed the Corn Laws of 1815, which were meant to assure a protected market for British agricultural interests. No foreign wheat could be imported into the British Isles unless the domestic price were to reach an exorbitantly high level. This condemned the low-income industrial workers of British towns and cities to a meager and expensive diet. The trade barriers also acted as restraints on the development of the emerging British manufacturing industries.

In 1820, a group of British industrialists issued a "Merchant's Petition" declaring that they were "against every restrictive regulation of trade, not essential to the revenue, against all duties merely protective from foreign competition." In 1830, Sir Henry Parnell, a long-time Chairman of the Finance Committee of the House of Commons, published *On Financial Reform*. In this book he declared, "If once men were allowed to take their own way, they would very soon, to the great advantage of society, undeceive the world of the error of restricting trade, and show that the passage of merchandise from one state to another ought to be as free as air and water. Every country should be as a general and common fair for the sale of goods, and the individual and nation which makes the best commodity should find the greatest advantage."[7]

In 1836, an Anti-Corn Law Association was formed in London, which in 1839 was renamed the Anti-Corn Law League in Manchester. For the next seven years, under the masterful and powerful leadership of Richard Cobden and John Bright, the League fought unstintingly for the repeal of the Corn Laws and the establishment of total free trade in the British Empire. Throughout the cities, towns, and villages of Great Britain Anti-Corn Law League chapters were opened. Hundreds of thousands of dollars were collected as voluntary donations to fund rallies, meetings, public lectures, and debates. They organized a vast publishing campaign of books, monographs, and pamphlets advocating the repeal of all protectionist restrictions and the freeing of all trade and commerce from government control.

From the beginning, Richard Cobden, in making his case for free trade, saw the breaking down of trade barriers as a powerful avenue for depoliticizing human relationships; by privatizing all market transactions between individuals of different countries, free trade would assist in removing many of the causes of war. "As little intercourse as possible between Governments," Cobden declared, "as much connection as possible between the nations of the world." To emphasize this, the slogan of the Anti-Corn Law League became "Free Trade, Peace, and Good-Will Among Nations."

Furthermore, Cobden and the Anti-Corn Law League made theirs the case for *unilateral* free trade: "We came to the conclusion that the less we attempted to persuade foreigners to adopt our trade principles, the better," Cobden explained in later years, "for we discovered so much suspicion of the motives of England, that it was lending an argument to the protectionists abroad to incite the popular feeling against the free-traders. . . . To take away this pretense, we avowed our total indifference whether other nations became free-traders or not; but we should abolish Protection for our own selves, and leave other countries to take whatever course they liked best."[8]

In 1841, Sir Robert Peel became Prime Minister; he was determined to maintain the Corn Laws as a cornerstone of British foreign economic policy. But through one of those ironies of history, the man appointed to lead the defense of protectionism ended up presiding over the abolition of protectionism in Great Britain. Over a period of years, Peel's government lowered and in some cases eliminated many of the trade restrictions on manufacturing and industrial goods, but it balked at reducing the trade barriers on agriculture. Under the unrelenting arguments of the free traders, Peel finally admitted, during a debate in the House of Commons in 1843, "I am bound to say that it is our interest to buy cheap, whether other countries will buy cheap or no." In 1845, of the 813 commodities on the import tariff restriction list, 430 were moved to the free trade list. But, still, Peel was unwilling to give way on the Corn Laws.

Then, in the fall of 1845, the worst rains in living memory hit the British Isles and the domestic food crops were devastated. Food supplies declined, bread prices rose dramatically, and the potato harvest was destroyed in Ireland, threatening mass starvation. Young boys could be heard in the cities saying, "I be protected and I be starving." Daniel O'Connell led demonstrations in Ireland in which a cannon would be dragged through the streets to which was attached a sign saying, "Free trade or this." In November 1845, the leaders of both the Tory and Whig parties came out for repeal of the Corn Laws. In January 1846, Robert Peel told the House of Commons that the Corn Laws would be abolished. On February 27, the resolution was approved, and the Corn Importation Bill left the House of Commons on May 16, after passing on the third reading. The Duke of Wellington speedily ushered the bill through the House of Lords, and free trade became the law of the land in Great Britain on June 26, 1846.

Angered by his surrender to the free traders, the protectionist Tories forced Robert Peel to resign from the prime ministership the very same day free trade was triumphant in Britain. In his final public address, Peel declared that he hoped that whatever government was formed it would continue the "application of those principles which tend to establish a freer intercourse with other nations." And he went on to say:

> If other countries choose to buy in the dearest market,
> such an option on their part constitutes no reason why
> we should not be permitted to buy in the cheapest. I trust
> the Government ... will not resume the policy which they
> and we have felt most inconvenient, namely, the haggling
> with foreign countries about reciprocal concessions, in-
> stead of taking the independent course which we believe
> conducive to our own interests. Let us trust to the influ-
> ence of public opinion in other countries—let us trust
> that our example, with the proof of practical benefit we
> derive from it, will at no remote period insure the adoption
> of the principles on which we have acted, rather than de-
> fer indefinitely by delay equivalent concessions from
> other countries.[9]

Within three years, by 1849, not only were the Corn Laws
gone, but so were the remaining Navigation Acts carried over
from the 18th century that had required goods being imported into Britain to be carried on British ships. From then on,
both goods and merchant vessels from any land could arrive
in Great Britain "as free as air and water," as Henry Parnell
had wished it to be in 1830.

One hundred and fifty years ago, on June 26, 1846, Great
Britain became the first country in the world to institute a
unilateral policy of free trade. For the rest of the 19th century, indeed, until the dark forces of collectivism enveloped
Europe during World War I, the British Empire was open to
all the world for the free movement of men, money, and goods.
Its economic success served as a bright, principled example
to the rest of the globe, many of whose member countries
followed the British lead in establishing, if not completely
free trade, at least regimes of much greater freedom of trade
and commerce.[10]

The triumph of free trade in 1846 in Great Britain was one
of the shining jewels in the crowning achievements of 19th-
century classical liberalism. But it represented not only the
opening of the door to material prosperity among an expanding

groups of nations of the world. It also heralded an epoch of greatly depoliticized relationships that, in fact, made international trade the private affairs of individuals and not concerns of the state.[11] What type of international order was created in those last decades of the 19th century under the increasing adoption free trade, free markets, low taxes, and limited government by more and more countries in the "civilized world" of Europe and North America? Here is one description, by the Austrian economist Oskar Morgenstern:

> Before 1914 there was freedom of travel without passports, freedom of migration, and freedom from exchange control and other monetary restrictions. Citizenship was freely granted to immigrants. Short-term or long-term capital could move unsupervised in any direction, and these movements took any form. Direct foreign investments were common and welcome; securities of other countries were freely traded on most stock markets. Trans-fer of profits was unhampered and foreign investments were not confiscated after they had begun to show yield. Monetary standards in most countries were firmly established in gold. . . . Indeed the monetary systems of some countries were tied together even more firmly by international monetary unions—for example, the Latin Union—organized so that the money of each member state could circulate freely at par in all other member states. Gold coins of all countries found their way easily in all directions. . . . It is also noteworthy that international financial and commercial transactions before 1914 were among individuals (and corporations) and rarely among countries dealing as a whole. . . . National boundaries were thus of small importance, as was the fact that most countries had different currencies. . . . There were colonial wars, but they did not leave deep scars. There were also other wars such as the Spanish–American, the Russo–Japanese, and the Balkan war, but they were localized and occurred at the periphery of economic centers.[12]

Collectivism, Full Employment, the Welfare State, and State Management of Global Trade

The emergence of socialism and neo-mercantilism toward the end of the 19th century eventually brought about the end of the classical liberal era and its epoch of free trade, free markets, and free men. Beginning in the 1880s, Imperial Germany led the way in bringing about the demise of free trade, with its establishment of the welfare state and its growing drive for territorial self-sufficiency.[13] The rest of the world followed suit during the First World War, when under the argument of war-time national emergencies, every one of the belligerent nations introduced trade barriers, migration restrictions, exchange controls, national planning, and abridgments of civil liberties. And the world never recovered from the repoliticizing of economic life during the Great War. The "return to normalcy" in the 1920s, both in the United States and in Europe, still left intact a heavy legacy of government controls, expanded welfare statism, and a new ideology of economic nationalism.[14] The Great Depression in the 1930s only intensified the growth of economic nationalistic tendencies in the general climate of political collectivism that dominated practically all the leading countries of the world.[15]

In the totalitarian countries of the interwar period (fascist Italy, Nazi Germany, and the Soviet Union) the ideology of collectivism dictated the repoliticizing of international trade. In the total state there was no domain of the private individual, untouchable by the supreme political authority. As Benito Mussolini clearly expressed it: "Against individualism, the Fascist conception is for the State.... Fascism reaffirms the State as the true reality of the individual.... Fascism is ... for the only liberty that can be a real thing, the liberty of the State. ... Therefore, for the Fascist, everything is in the State, and nothing human or spiritual exists, much less has value, outside the State. In this sense Fascism is totalitarian.... Outside of the State there can be neither individuals nor groups."[16]

In the Soviet Union, there could be no question of private trade, commerce, or international exchange; the government had nationalized all the means of production and placed them under the direct control of the central planning authority, which determined, in the interests of the "dictatorship of the proletariat," the importation and exportation of any commodities or raw materials in terms of whether or not it would serve the goals of the socialist state's "Plan." In fascist Italy and Nazi Germany, private trade, commerce, and exchange was made subordinate to the interests and goals of "the nation" or "the race," respectively, for the achievement of which the state dictated the direction of production, regulated wages and prices, and controlled the flows of imports and exports.

At the same time, while not having the same extreme political implications or consequences, the interventionist-regulated economy that came to dominate the major Western democracies in the 1930s meant that international trade could not be viewed as the private affairs of various individuals, either.[17] Governments were increasingly charged with responsibility for the maintenance and stability of various national aggregates—the levels of total employment, output, and wages and prices—within their respective national borders. Keynesian economics played a crucial role in cementing this conception of the role and responsibility of governments. It was argued, by Keynes and those who developed his theoretical edifice in the 1940s, that it was possible for governments through the right mix of monetary and fiscal policies to influence the levels of national employment and output. Maintaining sufficient "aggregate demand" to assure continuous "full employment" became the central principle advocated by proponents of the "new economics."

For the German-language edition of *The General Theory of Employment, Interest, and Money,* Keynes wrote a special foreword in September 1936. He told the economists of Nazi Germany that, "[T]he theory of output as a whole, which is what the following book purports to provide, is much more easily adopted to the conditions of a totalitarian state, than . . . under conditions of free competition and a large degree of laissez faire."[18] I am not suggesting that Keynes was a Nazi sympathizer or an advocate of totalitarianism: Such a charge would be extremely unjust. But I do suggest that Keynes did see very clearly that if his set of policy proposals for government monetary and fiscal intervention to maintain full employment was to work, then the market forces outside of government control or direct influence had to be kept to a minimum.

One primary market force that has the potential to undermine a national policy of full employment is international trade. Government attempts to increase aggregate demand and generate greater employment can be foiled by consumers, that is, if they are free to buy foreign goods that they find more attractive or less expensive than the domestic versions for sale. And the free entry of less expensive foreign commodities can undermine government attempts to maintain high domestic aggregate demand and artificially high wages and labor demands. Government attempts to stimulate domestic investment by artificially lowering interest rates through monetary expansion can also be blocked, if the savers and lenders in that country are at liberty to transfer their loanable funds to foreign markets where they can find interest rates higher than those now prevailing on the domestic market.[19]

If Keynesian "solutions" to supposed employment problems were to work, then governments needed to have within their authority the right to raise tariffs, control the quantity of imports and exports, restrict the free flow of financial capital across borders, and influence exchange rates between currencies. The more successfully the government could control any such private sector "leaks" out of the national economy, the greater the effect that government could hope to have over the aggregate levels of domestic output and employment. But the more the government extended its power over private sector choices and options concerning the direction of national economic activity, the narrower, necessarily, had to become the arena of strictly market-determined outcomes. And logically, therefore, the greater the "total" control by the state over that nation's economy. Keynes was quite right (and quite honest) when he told the Nazi economists of the mid-1930s that his policy prescriptions might be more effectively applied in their fascist version of the planned economy than in the increasingly regulated but still freer market economies of the Western democracies.[20]

Seymour Harris, one of the most ardent and prolific popularizers of Keynesian economics in the 1940s and 1950s, pointed out, "In the twenties, Keynes had made up his mind that independence in monetary policy was a *sine qua non* for sensible domestic policy; and that independence and laissez faire were not compatible. . . . [In the 1940s] he now said and reiterated that Great Britain would not subject its economy to controls from without; that a country pursuing prudent policies at home must not be embarrassed by strains originating abroad; that domestic policies of each country are the primary concern."[21]

It should be clear to critics, however, that if every country were to follow this policy prescription, government controls, regulations, and prohibitions on international trade would be the rule and not the exception. International trade frictions would be inevitable as each nation suspiciously watched the export and import policies of their neighbors for signs of danger to their respective domestic policies goals.

But the global expansion of the welfare state earlier in this century also required the repoliticizing of international trade. The essence of the welfare state is the redistribution of wealth. The welfare state includes direct income transfers between various groups in the society; state provision of retirement plans and health-care insurance and services; in-kind provision by the state of various goods and services to eligible groups in the society; the guaranteeing or influencing of various relative income shares earned by different groups in the society through minimum wage laws, regulatory practices, licensing procedures, workplace health and safety standards, subsidies and direct government expenditures for various goods and services. And these are just a few of the methods and goals in a welfare state! International trade can undermine or weaken the ability of the state to fulfill any number of these redistributive purposes. Every one of these programs requires massive amounts of tax revenues and detailed regulatory practices. Taxes siphon off private sector wealth that otherwise could have been used for savings, investment, and capital formation. It retards private capacities for research and development or, through government spending, redirects research and development away from strictly market-determined channels into those to which the government assigns greater political importance. Minimum wage laws, workplace health and safety rules, and regulatory restraints and procedures for the manufacture and sale of goods and services all reduce market flexibility and responsiveness to changing circumstances, both in the domestic and international market.

The implementation of the "safety net society," both in terms of government provision of "social programs" and government guarantees of protected relative income shares, cannot be as fully assured if international trade is free and unrestricted. Goods may come in that out-compete minimum wage sectors of the economy; foreign goods may incorporate technologies and features attractive to the buying public, but which the domestic producers cannot readily match. Why? Because taxes have prevented the accumulation of the savings that could have enabled relevant private sector research and development. Or because research and development is now found to have been shunted down a wrong track due to government influence on the direction taken by R&D. Or because domestic producers' shares of their nation's market may be reduced because the regulatory rules and procedures diminish their ability to match their foreign competitors' offerings to the consumers of that society. And this, in turn, can affect government welfare spending and tax receipts if, in the face of loss of market share, sectors of the domestic economy must "downsize." At the same time, alternative employment and investment opportunities will not be easily found or moved into precisely because the marketplace rules, regulations, and restrictions imposed by the interventionist–welfare state preclude relatively rapid adjustment to the changed circumstances of domestic and global supply and demand.[22]

During World War II, the Allied countries, led by the United States, decided that a return to the autarkic and beggar-thy-neighbor policies of the period between both world wars would be a disaster. International trade and commerce, global access to raw materials, and the opportunity for foreign investment were considered essential elements if a new world order was to be constructed; this new world order was planned to be superior to the economic nationalism of the interwar period.[23]

But the new world order that arose out of the ashes of World War II was not like the world order before 1914. The new international economic order was not grounded in the older classical liberal notion of free trade. As the German free market economist Moritz Bonn pointed out in 1945, "International economic relations can be carried out in three different ways: exclusively by private individuals and corporations; exclusively by governments; or by private persons and corporations on the one side and by governments and government institutions on the other side."[24] Before World War I, while not completely free of government control and influence, international commerce and trade had predominantly been the affairs of private individuals.[25] In the period between the wars, international trade had fallen extensively under government control.[26] In the post-World War II period, international trade became an admittedly fairly liberal, but nonetheless intergovernmental, system of managed and controlled trade.[27]

The global economy was based upon and managed in the context of a set of international governmental organizations. The late David Osterfeld summarized this political order of international economic relations:

> The three pillars of the postwar economic world were the World Bank, intended to make long-term loans for the reconstruction of a Europe ravaged by war and to Third World countries to stimulate economic development by the creation of wealth; the International Monetary Fund, designed to insure monetary stability through the use of short-term loans; and the General Agreement on Tariffs and Trade, whose purpose was to promote an open international trading order. Together, it was thought, the three institutions would prevent a return to the economic nationalism that characterized the depression years of the 1930s when many nations engaged in "competitive depreciation" of their currencies in order to stimulate exports while enacting tariffs in an effort to prevent imports, thereby, it was hoped, stimulating domestic production and reducing unemployment.[28]

What was the consequence in the post-war era? Looking back on the three decades after 1945, Gottfried Haberler stated, "There is virtually general agreement that the first twenty-five or thirty years after World War II were a period of unprecedented growth and prosperity. Compared with the interwar period, the entire postwar period . . . must be judged a great success. . . . World trade grew by leaps and bounds."[29] And it is the continuing legacy of that fairly liberal system of managed trade that is the basis for the continuation in the growth of trade and investment outlined in the opening section of this essay.

But beginning in the 1970s, the general trend began to be away from more liberal and freer trade to greater controlled and managed trade. The methods employed were less the traditional ones of tariff barriers and import restrictions, and more of a different kind. The techniques were explained by Jan Tumlir in the 1980s:

> The new protectionism is a very different animal. It has been growing gradually. Industries have used intelligent, long-term planning creating an expanded system of protection. The expansion proceeds sectorially; instead of an effort to reduce all imports as much as possible, we are witnessing the construction of industrial protection systems, each tailored to the special needs of the industry in question, each administered by a highly specialized bureaucracy, often co-opted into public service from the respective industry association. The system coordinates several instruments—trade restrictions, subsidies, explicit or tacit exemptions from competition or antitrust law, and elements of direct government regulation. The protectionism of the 1930s was openly adversary; the new one, however, builds on negotiations, indeed, is in a perverse way the result of international cooperation. As a result, the new protectionism is politically stronger because it accommodates a broader range of interests. Where earlier forms of protection created vested interests in the importing country only, the new protectionism has built up almost equally strong vested interest on the export side as well. . . . For all these reasons the new protectionism will be much more difficult to roll back.[30]

How has this trend come about? It is explained primarily by the factors discussed earlier. While proclaiming a belief in free trade and globalized commerce, the world in the post-war period increasingly became enveloped in the spider's web of welfare statist programs that required governments to secure redistributive shares of income and market shares for selected and privileged sectors of their respective economies. Given the institutional responsibilities that modern governments have taken upon themselves in the name of the "social good," the "national interest," and the "general welfare" as the 20th century has progressed, and most especially during the last six decades, the state's use of both domestic as well as international policy tools to serve special interests feeding at the trough of the government has been inevitable.[31]

The international institutions established after 1945 have reflected this ideological, political, and economic trend. Whether it be the International Monetary Fund (IMF), the World Bank, or the General Agreement on Tariffs and Trade (transformed in 1995 into the World Trade Organization), the purpose has been for governments to oversee, manage, and direct the pattern of international trade and investment. The IMF and the World Bank have expanded and extended their activities to more greatly influence the distribution of loanable funds to both governments and private investors, especially in Third World countries. They have also taken upon themselves the responsibility of tying such loans and credits to guidelines for economic policy reform in the recipient nations. During their five-decade histories, the IMF and the World Bank have followed the various interventionist and collectivist fads and fashions that have dominated public policy, whether in the industrialized countries or the Third World nations: financial support of nationalized industries, below-market interest rate loans for loss-making sectors of the economy, billion-dollar credit lines for Third World governments, sponsorship of land and income redistribution, planning schemes to foster "balanced growth," and balanced-budget plans that tie IMF and World Bank money to tax increases.[32]

As we saw during the first several decades of international trade relations under the General Agreement on Tariffs and Trade (GATT), global commerce was noticeably liberalized, with tariff barriers and import restrictions being significantly lowered. Yet, this was not been the result of free trade but rather of the particular pattern of politically managed trade agreed upon by the leading international trading players. It remained in effect only for as long as the member governments in this international organization continued to regulate the global market in the direction of freer trade.

Since the 1970s, however, the world has increasingly come to be dominated by a different set of ideas about the circumstances when international trade can be considered "fair" and "just."[33] The central problem with an idea like "fair trade" is that it is as empty and ambiguous a term as "social justice," being able to mean almost anything that the user of the concept wishes it to.[34] As Jagdish Bhagwati has pointed out, under the heading of "fair trade" nearly anything that one country does in terms of its domestic and trading policies can be rationalized by another government as involving "unfair" trade practices that negatively affect or threaten its domestic industries' market circumstances. "If everything becomes a question of fair trade," Professor Bhagwati has pointed out, " 'Managed trade' will then be the outcome, with bureaucrats allocating trade according to what domestic lobbying pressures and foreign political muscle dictate."[35]

Will the new World Trade Organization (WTO)—which is an outgrowth of the GATT—be any better? The preamble of the agreement establishing the WTO states that the joint purpose of the member governments is to "raise standards of living, ensuring full employment and a large and steadily growing volume of real income and effective demand, and expanding the production of and trade in goods and services, while allowing for optimal use of the world's resources in accordance with the objective of sustainable development, seeking both to protect and preserve the environment and to enhance the means of doing so in a manner consistent with their respective needs and concerns at different levels of development."[36]

In the WTO's own summary of its duties and responsibilities as an international institution representing the member governments of the world, it is stated that "The WTO is not the 'free-trade' institution it is sometimes described as—if only because it permits tariffs and, in limited circumstances, other forms of protection. It is more accurate to say it is a system of rules dedicated to open, fair, and undistorted competition. ... The WTO agreement on agriculture [for example] is designed to provide fairness in farm trade." And as a carryover of previous GATT provisions, "industrial countries" are "encouraged" to "assist developing nation members 'as a matter of conscious and purposeful effort' in their trading conditions." In other words, the WTO is delegated the responsibility to oversee the negotiation and administration of international trade agreements that have the task of reconciling the irreconcilable: the liberalization of international trade relations among the nations of the world in the political-economic context of national policies of welfare-statism, interventionism, protectionism, and indicative planning to foster the maintenance and growth of privileged industrial and agricultural sectors of the respective national economies of the various member nations. All that can be expected from the WTO, therefore, is a continuation of the same types of policies that have up until now stood in the way of an actual international order of liberal free trade.

The World Trade Organization is headquartered in Geneva, Switzerland, at 154, rue de Lausanne, at the Centre William Rappard. It is highly probable that most of the executives and employees at the WTO know very little about the ideas of the man in whose name the building in which their offices are housed has been dedicated. Yet William Rappard, an economist and political scientist by training (and a long-time friend of Ludwig von Mises), was one of the most knowledgeable and respected proponents of individual freedom, free trade, and democratic government in the period between the two world wars. In numerous writings he explained the disastrous consequences that must always result from collectivism, totalitarianism, economic nationalism, and protectionism.[37]

In one of his finest essays, "The Common Menace of Economic and Military Armaments," delivered in London as the Richard Cobden Lecture of 1936, after lucidly demonstrating all of the dangers and costs of economic nationalism and political collectivism, William Rappard concluded that "the only hope of humanity therefore lies in a return to the Cobdenite ideals of individual freedom within each nation, and of economic cooperation, peace, and goodwill among all nations."[38] He believed that a return to a regime of limited government and free enterprise was the only true path to a world in which the individual would be secure in his liberty against that greatest threat to human freedom: the state. In his brilliant 1938 book summarizing the history of democracy through the ages and the totalitarian threats it faced in the 20th century, Rappard explained why economic freedom was so important. If political freedom was to be preserved and restored, he argued,

> ... Our efforts would tend to relieve the state of many of the burdens under which it is staggering today and under which it cannot remain either responsive to the will of the people or respectful of their primary liberties. As we see it, the defense of democracy demands a return to greater economic freedom, without which no state, however organized, can give its citizens more than the illusion of governing themselves. If the political will of the people is again to become supreme, it must be content to assert itself over a more limited domain. It is, therefore, not only because we believe private enterprise to be more creative, more progressive, more efficient, and consequently productive of greater general prosperity than that of the state, that we venture to advocate a limitation of the latter. It is also because we believe that no state that has been allowed to become totalitarian in its activities can fail to become totalitarian in its claims on the subservience of its subjects. Our plea for more private liberty is, therefore, political no less than economic.[39]

With the end of the Soviet Union in 1991, the world saw the end of the last of the totalitarian states that originally emerged out of the wreckage of World War I. Democratic government has ended the 20th century triumphant against all the earlier collectivist and totalitarian rationales for denying people representative participation in the political process. Yet the collectivist premises still dominate domestic and international economic policy, as is clearly enunciated in the preamble to the establishment of the WTO: Governments are responsible for increasing standards of living, full employment, rising real income, environmental regulation, "optimal" resource use, and "sustainable development." International trade is to be pursued and regularized among the nations of the world in the context of each country pursuing these stated national objectives. Both individual freedom and a peaceful, open regime of free trade are to be subservient to these interventionist and welfare-statist goals.

In a 1937 essay, Rappard defined nationalism as "the doctrine which places the nation at the top of the scale of political values, that is above the three rival values of the individual, of regional units, and of the international community. . . . If we wished to define economic nationalism by its underlying purpose, we should say that it was a doctrine destined to serve the nation by making it not richer, but freer, by promoting not its material welfare, but its independence of foreign influences."[40] By this definition, while not totalitarian in its compass, the world is still ruled by economic nationalism. For as demonstrated earlier, once the state takes on responsibility for income maintenance and redistribution, welfare state "safety nets," secured market shares for both its domestic and foreign trade sectors, and the growth of industries earmarked for privileged subsidized development—all national goals within the confines of the boundaries of the nation-state—it by necessity places these goals above the liberty of its own individual citizens and an open international order. Until these last vestiges of collectivism and nationalism are set aside, the attainment of a real global economic system will be impossible. And it is clear that the World Trade Organization, based on its own statement of purpose, represents little of the fundamental political-economic principles of individual liberty and free trade that were advocated by the man in whose name the building is dedicated in which the WTO has its headquarters.[41]

A Free Global Economy for the 21st Century

In 1927, Ludwig von Mises wrote:

> [Classical] liberalism is, from the very outset, a world-embracing political concept, and the same ideas that it seeks to realize within a limited area it holds to be valid also for the larger sphere of world politics. . . . The starting point of [classical] liberal thought is the recognition of the value and importance of human cooperation. . . . The ultimate ideal envisioned by [classical] liberalism is the perfect cooperation of all mankind, taking place peacefully and without friction. [Classical] liberal. . . . thinking is cosmopolitan and ecumenical, it takes in all men and the whole world. [Classical] liberalism is, in this sense, humanism; and the [classical] liberal, a citizen of the world, cosmopolite.[42]

The good news for classical liberals today is that the last vestiges of collectivism and interventionist-welfare statism that continue to hold the world in its grip have lost their ideological and philosophic underpinnings. The brave new worlds promised by communism, fascism, and Nazism—and in pursuit of which the 20th century was made a brutal nightmare for millions of people—have lost their euphoric appeals. The interventionist-welfare state that grew out of a general acceptance of the Marxian and socialist critique of capitalist society has been reduced to a financially crushing political game of special-interest politics for privilege and redistributive favors.[43] The contemporary political rhetoric about racism, genderism, and environmentalism is merely the latest variation on the old Marxism theme of "class conflict," i.e., sup-

posed irreconcilabilities between groups—racial groups, sex-
ual groups, man vs. animal, and plant-life groups.[44]

It is time to go beyond these reactionary, anti-individualist
ideas of the recent past. It is time to pick up the threads of
the ideas of classical liberalism that were broken by the opening
shots of World War I. A better, freer, more prosperous world
can be ours. What would such a world look like? Mises once
gave an outline of such a free world, and it is worth quoting
it at length:

> [Classical] liberalism's proposals for the coexistence and
> cooperation of nations and states are only a part of the
> total [classical] liberal program. They can be realized,
> they can be made to work only within a [classical] liber-
> al world. The main excellence of the [classical] liberal
> scheme of social, economic, and political organization is
> precisely this—it makes the peaceful cooperation of na-
> tions possible. . . .
>
> In order to grasp the meaning of this liberal program
> we need to imagine a world order in which [classical]
> liberalism is supreme. Either all the states in it are [clas-
> sical] liberal, or enough are so that when united they are
> able to repulse an attack of militarist aggressors. In this
> [classical] liberal world, or [classical] liberal part of the
> world, there is private property in the means of produc-
> tion. The working of the market is not hampered by gov-
> ernment interference. There are no trade barriers; men
> can live and work where they want. Frontiers are drawn
> on the maps but they do not hinder the migrations of
> men and shipping of commodities. Natives do not enjoy
> rights that are denied to aliens. Governments and their
> servants restrict their activities to the protection of life,
> health, and property against fraudulent or violent aggres-
> sion. They do not discriminate against foreigners. The
> courts are independent and effectively protect everybody
> against the encroachments of officialdom. Everyone is

permitted to say, to write, and to print what he likes. Education is not subject to government interference. Governments are like night-watchmen whom the citizens have entrusted with the task of handling the police power. The men in office are regarded as mortal men, not as superhuman beings or paternal authorities who have the right and the duty to hold the people in tutelage. Governments do not have the right to dictate to the citizens what language they must use in their daily speech or in what language they must bring up or educate their children. Administrative organs and tribunals are bound to use each man's language in dealing with him, provided this language is spoken in the district by a reasonable number of residents.

In such a world it makes no difference where the frontiers of a country are drawn. Nobody has a special material interest in enlarging the territory of the state in which he lives; nobody suffers a loss if a part of this area is separated from the state. It is also immaterial whether all parts of the state's territory are in direct geographical connection, or whether they are separated by a piece of land belonging to another state. It is of no economic importance whether the county has frontage on the ocean or not.... For [classical] liberalism there is no problem here at all. Private railroads, if quite free of government interference, can traverse the territory of many states without any trouble. If there are no tariff boundaries and no limitations on the movement of persons, animals, or goods, then it is of no consequence whether a train ride in a few hours crosses the borders of [several] states more or less often.... An inland country believes that it needs a "corridor" to the sea in order to keep its foreign trade free of the influence of the interventionist and [statist] policies of the countries whose territories separate it from the sea. If free trade were the rule, it would be hard to see what advantage an inland country could expect from the possession of a "corridor.". . .

There would be no more wars because there would be no incentive for aggression. War would not pay. Armies and navies would be superfluous. Policeman would suffice for the fight against crime. In such a world the state is not a metaphysical entity but simply the producer of security and peace. It is the night-watchman. . . .

The reality in which we have to live differs very much from this perfect world of ideal [classical] liberalism. But this is due only to the fact that men have rejected [classical] liberalism for [statism]. They have burdened the state, which could be a more or less efficient night-watchman, with a multitude of other duties. Neither nature, nor the working of forces beyond human control, nor inevitable necessity has led to [statism], but the acts of men.[45]

If Mises's imagery of a perfect world of ideal classical liberalism seems "radical" and "politically impossible" or "realistically unattainable," it is worth remembering, as we saw, that in its essence that was the world before World War I. Not perfect and not as "pure" as outlined as an ideal by Mises, but very close, and certainly a lot closer than what most of the world has experienced in the 20th century.[46]

How can we return to freedom's road in the 21st century? We must dismantle the interventionist–welfare state and all of the institutions upon which it is maintained.

The Dismantling of the Welfare State as a Precondition for a Liberal International Order

The welfare state is unreformable and can never be made compatible with a civil society of peaceful and voluntary human relationships. It is in its essence what the 19th-century French free market economist Frederic Bastiat called a system of "legalized plunder," in which the wealth and income of one segment of society is forcibly redistributed to another segment of society as the unending product of a war of all-against-all between special interest groups of sundry sorts in the arena of democratic politics.[47]

It is vital to revive an historical memory of how, in the 19th and early 20th centuries, it was the private sector that developed charitable and for-profit methods to alleviate the human problems of a complex and changing society that in our time are considered to require intrusions by the state into the private and interpersonal affairs of the citizenry.[48] Indeed, it was only following the emergence of the state's growing intrusion into these matters that the private sector was increasingly "crowded out"; the private sector was unable to match the government's "unfair competition" of being about to offer the provision of these "social" services at zero or heavily subsidized prices by taxing the general public and, at the same time, depriving the private sector of the financial resources needed to continue to offer alternative charitable options in the magnitudes required.

Furthermore, there can be no lasting hope for the development of a international order of open, free trade for as long as the state makes the provision and maintenance of such programs matters of fundamental "national interest." As the German free market economist Wilhelm Röpke clearly explained, the welfare state is a major creator and reinforcer of the nationalist spirit that runs counter to such an international order:

> Since the national government is both the organizer of welfare and the compulsive agent, the fact that economic and social life become objects of political action means that they are nationalized themselves, which, in turn, means that an excessive social integration grows up within the framework of the national state, making all the more difficult the process of international integration. The more frequently appeals are made to the "solidarity"

of people who share the same passport or the same national residence the more they are forced into a self-supporting, economically isolationist "national community," the more complete is the "nationalization" of human beings at the expense of the free international community of nations and of international solidarity.... While saving and private insurance are forms of provision which belong to the sphere of economics, the market, private law and freedom, and are not, therefore, confined by national boundaries, public provision belongs to the realm of politics, collectivist organization, public law and compulsion and, therefore, tends to lock people up within their national boundaries.[49]

The Abolition of the Regulated Economy as a Precondition for a Liberal International Order

When the classical liberals and free market economists in the early and middle decades of the 19th century advocated the dismantling of the 18th century system of economic controls and regulations known as mercantilism, it was not only because they believed that such an interventionist system was incompatible with the individual's right of free, peaceful interaction with his fellow men for mutually beneficial gain. They also argued that no government, or its administrative officials, had the knowledge or ability to order and direct the affairs of private citizens better than those private persons could do for themselves. And, furthermore, they argued that the productive results of free men interacting in pursuit of their respective self-interests would generate a greater and more widely dispersed wealth of nations than under any state supervision.[50]

In our century, the interventionist system has returned in a much more comprehensive form than ever experienced before the triumph of free trade in the mid-19th century. Every facet of market activity is under the regulation, licensing, and approval of the state. In the political arena, economic regulation has become the primary mechanism for those who wish to limit or eliminate competition in their respective corners of the market.[51] Furthermore, the economic theories that predominantly underlie the rationales for government regulation present a distorted understanding of the actual, dynamic market process out of which arises the creative entrepreneurial competition that generates the continual coordination of supply and demand, as well as a never-ending stream of new and improved goods and services for the consuming public.[52]

In addition, the greater the extent of domestic regulation, the more unrestricted foreign competition threatens to undermine the goals for which the regulations have been established in the first place—and the more the state must oppose free trade. This has been explained with great clarity by Mises:

> A nation's policy forms an integral whole. Foreign policy and domestic policy are closely linked together, they are but one system. Economic nationalism is the corollary of the present-day domestic policies of government interference with business and national planning as free trade was the complement of domestic free trade. There can be protectionism in a country with domestic free trade, but where there is no domestic free trade, protectionism is indispensable. A national government's might is limited to the territory subject to its sovereignty. It does not have the power to interfere directly with conditions abroad. Where there is free trade, foreign competition would in the short run already frustrate the aims sought by the various measures of government intervention with domestic business. When the domestic market is not to some extent insulated from the foreign markets, there can be no question of government control. The farther a nation goes on the way to public regulation and regimentation, the more it is pushed toward economic isolation.[53]

A Sound Monetary System as a Precondition for a Liberal International Order

In the 19th century, classical liberals considered the gold standard as the monetary corollary to free trade and free markets. Having experienced the harmful consequences of paper money and inflation during the Napoleonic Wars, the classical liberals were extremely suspicious of allowing governments unrestrained and discretionary control over money. By limiting the issuance of paper money to a fixed ratio of the gold left on deposit in banks, the classical liberals believed that a check would be placed on the possibility of an over-issue of depreciating currency. A sound monetary system, they argued, would serve as the financial backdrop for savings, investment, and capital formation. And, indeed, the gold standard of the 19th and early 20th centuries served just that valuable role. As Melchior Palyi explained:

> The gold standard was "sacrosanct" to the generations brought up on the Adam Smith ideals of free markets, from arbitrary and discriminatory interventions of governmental powers. Indeed, it was an essential instrument of economic freedom. It protected the individual against arbitrary measures of the government by offering a convenient hedge against "confiscatory" taxation, as well as against the depreciation of devaluation of the currency. It was an instrument of "mobility" within and beyond national borders. Above all, it raised a mighty barrier against authoritarian interferences with the economic process. . . . The gold standard in the classical sense was part and parcel of an economic order. It was a keystone of the system of public law, social customs and institutions, called "capitalism". . . a system that rested on what appears in perspective as virtually unlimited freedom of consumer choice, business enterprise, and markets. . . . The role of gold in unifying the economy of the civilized world can scarcely

be overestimated. It was the condition *sine qua non* of the international capital flow, both short-term and long-term, a basic instrument in "opening up" the world to economic progress and diffusing modern civilization.[54]

The gold standard was destroyed by governments in the 20th century. First during World War I, as each of the belligerent powers wanted the unlimited power of printing money to finance their respective war expenditures, and then during the early 1930s as most of the major European and North American governments wanted, again, unlimited power to issue paper money as a panacea to "cure" the mass unemployment and falling industrial production experienced during the Great Depression.[55] All of the major countries of the world became practitioners of *monetary nationalism.*

Under the gold standard, each nation's currency was linked to the world supply of gold and its distribution among various countries.[56] The world's supply of gold was determined by the profitability of mining gold, given the monetary and nonmonetary uses for the metal relative to the costs of mining it out of the ground. The distribution of the world's supply of gold among the nations of the world was determined by the demands for the metal in various parts of the world as reflected in its price. If the demand for gold—for whatever purposes—increased or decreased in any particular country, this set in motion a change in its distribution, with gold moving into the country in which its value had risen and flowing out of the country in which (in comparison) its value was now lower. Prices and wages tended to rise in the country into which gold flowed, and prices and wages would tend to decline in that country out of which the gold was moving. The long-term movement of gold would continue until prices had sufficiently risen in one country and declined in the other country to again create a condition of equilibrium: That is, the purchasing power of a unit of gold over goods and services would be more or less equivalent in both countries. As a result, there no longer would exist any profit incentive for moving gold from one country to the other.

This is what made the gold standard an *international* monetary system. The various currencies and price structures of the major countries of the world were interconnected and interdependent with each other through their use of gold as the common "anchor" of the respective national currencies. This what made the gold standard relatively independent of the changing currents and influences of national politics. As long as a country was on the gold standard and the government of that country followed "the rules of the game" (of only expanding or contracting the quantity of its currency and bank deposit money in circulation to reflect any increases and decreases in the quantity of gold in that nation's economy), then that government had no or very limited direct monetary control over the structure of prices and wages in its country.

But it was precisely this monetary control that governments wanted, especially beginning in the 1930s. The major governments of the world, including the United States, discarded the gold standard and its limitations for the purpose of instituting *national monetary planning*. Governments wanted the authority to manipulate the quantity of money in circulation so as to have the power to try to "plan" the optimal level of prices and wages in the name of stimulating industrial expansion and full employment. And governments have continued this usurpation of authority over money in their national economies ever since. Such usurpation creates regimes of monetary nationalism, because the primary influence on both the level of, and any movements in, prices and wages in general in the various countries of the world are then controlled by the respective monetary central planners.[57]

To the extent to which the respective national currencies of the world are still interconnected, this is now a matter of the various governments of the world agreeing to set limits on the movements in the foreign exchange rates between their respective currencies and to follow various domestic monetary and fiscal policies to set floors and ceilings on their respective rates of monetary expansion.

The national monetary central planners may choose on their own, or in mutual agreement with their governmental partners in other countries, to follow a conservative policy that prevents the expansion of their respective national currencies to a point at which serious inflationary processes are set in motion; but if this is done, it is completely dependent upon the decisions of the political policymakers. There no longer exists an external check to limit monetary expansions in the same way as under the old pre-World War I gold standard.[58]

If it has generally come to be accepted that the end of communism and "the great socialist experiment" in the Soviet Union demonstrated the unworkability and failure of economic central planning in general, why should it be thought that it is in the wisdom and power of governments (or their designated administrative agencies) to succeed in carrying out *monetary central planning*? Because that is what government management of national monetary systems really is in its essence. The government decides what shall be legally designated money. The government plans the quantity of money that shall be in circulation in the national economy. It is the government, based on various policy objectives, that sets targets for what it thinks the trend in prices and wages should be; and what the level of (at least, short-term) interest rates should be, as intermediary steps to influencing investment, employment, and production in the economy. Governments have neither the knowledge nor the dispassionate rationality to successfully do these things, any more than the central planners in Moscow had the knowledge or ability to successfully plan the production and distribution of shoes, hats, or milk.

The classical liberal agenda for the 21st century, therefore, must include a vision of a nongovernmental monetary order. The monetary order of the future should be based on a market-generated system of free banking; a free banking system would replace government central banking and with it end any government control of the money supply.[59] With the end of central banking would also come the end of monetary nationalism. The monetary system will have been privatized, with the normal market forces of supply and demand determining which commodity is selected as the money-good (most likely gold and/or silver, if history is any judge); the market-determined profitability of the commodity's production, worldwide, would establish the quantity of the commodity supplied for monetary purposes. Governments would no longer have the power or the authority to manipulate the monetary standard in the name of national economic goals. In its place would arise a new monetary internationalism, a system that could generate the sound monetary foundation for a new century of global trade and prosperity.

Unilateral Free Trade as an Avenue for Moving Toward the New Global Economy of the Future

Can a classical liberal global order be created in a political environment in which the governments of the world all practice in various ways, for various purposes, a vast array of interventionist-welfare statist policies? Must the first steps toward such a free trade global economy for the 21st century wait until a sizable number of countries all come to the same political-philosophical and political-economic conclusions more or less simultaneously, so that the necessary policies can all be implemented at the same time and to the same extent across several international borders?

Quite simply, no. The British free traders of the 19th century set themselves the goals of opening the British Isles to unregulated free markets and free trade, in spite and regardless of the fact that all the other nations with which Great Britain traded and competed had chosen to retain their mercantilist and protectionist barriers against open international commerce.

Every lowering of a tariff or import restriction immediately benefits the consumers of the importing country. Goods bought at a higher price because of the previous import duty now are purchased for less. Depending on how elastic the demand is for the foreign goods at the lower per-unit price, consumers may now either spend more or less than before on the larger quantities purchased. If the demand is fairly inelastic, consumers will buy more, but their total expenditures on these goods will be less. This will leave more dollars in their pockets to increase their demand for things that they could not afford when the imported goods were sold at the past higher tariff prices. If consumer demand is fairly elastic, when the larger quantities of these goods are purchased at the lower free trade prices total consumer expenditures will be greater for these goods; the additional revenues earned by the foreign sellers will increase their financial ability to demand buy more American exports. Either way, the result is the outcome of the free market choices of the American consuming public. And either way, demand for American goods goes up, either due to an increased demand by Americans now that they have saved some money on less expensive imports or because of the increased demand of foreign sellers who now have a greater dollar income with which to purchase American goods.

What if the government of the other country now selling more exports to America keeps its trade barriers in place and won't allow their own citizens to import more American goods? Then the dollars they have earned will either be kept in the United States and used for direct or indirect investments in the American economy or those dollars will be sold to someone on the foreign exchange market who is interested in acquiring dollars precisely because he wishes either to buy American goods or to invest in the American economy. Either way, markets are benefited in the U.S.

What if the United States opens its borders to unrestricted trade and the government of another country decides to

take advantage of this by subsidizing some privileged industries so they can sell more in the U.S. at prices below the actual
market costs-of-production? The effect for the American
consumer is the same as if the foreign manufacturer had an
actual lowering of its costs-of-production: the good is available for less, the American buyers can purchase more and maybe
save some money in the process. Some domestic American
manufacturers may see a falling off in their business due to
this lower-cost foreign competition, but there is always work
to be done and investments that can be profitably undertak-
en, if only those who have capital to invest and if those who
have hands to hire are willing to adjust their activities to reflect
the changed market conditions. Who should complain about
the subsidized exports to the United States? Surely it should
be the taxpayers in the country providing those subsidies to
selected and privileged segments of the foreign country's
industries. It is those foreign taxpayers who suffer a redistribution of their income and wealth to the privileged special
interest groups in their own country.

What if another country, in spite of our own free trade policy, decides to raise its tariffs and import restrictions against
American goods? This may well reduce the market for and
sales of American goods in that country, resulting in lowered
profitability and diminished employment opportunities in the
affected export sectors of the U.S. economy. But what is to be
done? Retaliate and raise the import duties on that country's
goods that are sold in the U.S.? What are the consequences?
The foreign exporters now earn less from sales because Americans purchase a smaller amount at the raised tariff price; this,
in turn, means that those foreign manufacturers buy fewer
American exports because their dollar earning will have gone
down due to our retaliatory conduct. At the same time, it is the
American consumer who pays the higher price for the imported goods now that the tariff has been raised. American
exporters lose business and the American consumer is poorer to the extent of the increase of the tariff.

A hundred years ago, in 1896, British economist Henry Dunning MacLeod analyzed the consequences of retaliatory trade policies, using an example in which France is presumed to raise its tariffs against British goods and then Britain retaliates by raising its tariffs against French goods. He picturesquely concluded: "By the method of retaliatory duties, when the Frenchman smites us on one cheek, we immediately hit ourselves an extremely hard slap on the other. The Frenchman, by his duties, does us an injury, and we, by retaliating, immediately do ourselves a great deal more." MacLeod suggested that "the *true way to fight hostile tariffs is by free trade.*"[60]

Can the United States end its regulations of or subsidies to sectors of the American economy in a world in which other governments continue to regulate and subsidize? Regulatory intervention harms no one other than: (a) the American manufacturer, who is hindered or prevented from investing or utilizing his financial and real capital in ways he thinks would most likely earn him profits from better producing and marketing goods which he believes consumers desire and for which they would be willing to pay; and, (b) the American consumer, who is prevented from having the variety of goods and competitive alternatives that an open, unhampered market would tend to provide. To the extent that such regulatory or licensing restrictions are repealed the American market is made potentially more open, responsive, and productive in an ever-changing environment of shifting supply and demand, including in the arena of international trade.

The elimination of subsidies to all sectors of the American economy will immediately change the configuration of profitable investments and resource uses, from those artificially created by the government's distortion of prices and costs through the subsidy programs into a pattern of investment and resource utilization that reflects the actual market opportunities at home and abroad. And this can only improve the efficiency with which resources are applied, goods are manufactured, and consumer wants are satisfied.

To the extent that other nations subsidize selected industries for purposes of advancing research and technological development, the American manufacturer is saved part of the costs he might otherwise have had to incur. The American manufacturer can "jump into the market" on the back of the foreign developer who, through the tax dollars dispersed to that sector of the foreign economy, has "worked out" the bugs and refined the technological potentials. Any investments in similar or improved technologies the American competitor finds it privately profitable to pursue will therefore have the potential to be a more cost-efficient and improved version. Rather than being left behind because a foreign government is subsidizing various "high-tech" sectors of its economy, the American competitor can potentially leap ahead, not burdened with real capital incorporating the earlier versions that are being made obsolete with each new turn of the research and production experimentation process.

From practically every angle, therefore, the United States could follow a path of unilateral free trade and reap the benefits from doing so both in the short and the long run. Furthermore, the advantage of following such a unilateral course is that America's pace of progress toward free trade would not be controlled by or confined within the context of multilateral agreements of reciprocal tariff and other trade barrier reductions.

The United States hurts no other nation by going its own way. The governments of other nations can choose to buy high and sell low; they can surround their own citizens with protectionist walls that retard improvements in their standards of living; they can impose onerous taxes on their people in the pursuit of privileges and subsidies for some at the expense of others; they can conjure up any ideological fantasies they want to rationalize their economically irrational policies as a means to justify their actions to the citizens who must endure and bear the costs of what they do.

The example that we could create by pursuing a policy of unilateral free trade and radically liberated markets at home could serve as the same type of model for the world in the 21st century that Great Britain's heroic jump into unilateral free trade did for Europe and North America in the 19th century. In the late 1840s, Nassau Senior, one of the most respected British economists of his time, argued that:

> For centuries, the government has labored to fetter and misdirect the industry of the people. Instead of confining itself to its true task of defending its subjects from foreign and domestic violence and fraud, it has taken on itself the task of rendering them, or of rendering certain classes of them, rich. It has dictated to them what they shall produce, and to whom they shall sell, and what they shall purchase, and to whom they shall buy, and what they shall purchase, and to what markets they shall resort. It has considered the whole body of consumers as a prey to be sacrificed to any class, or to any section of a class, that chose to ask for a monopoly....
>
> The advocate of freedom dwells on the benefit of making full use of our own particular advantages of situation, wealth, and skill, and availing ourselves to the utmost of those possessed by our neighbors.... He observes, in the words of Adam Smith, that is the maxim of every prudent master of a family, never to make at home what it will cost him more to make than to buy. The tailor does not make his own shoes, but buys them of the shoemaker. The shoemaker does not make his own clothes, but buys them of the tailor. The farmer attempts to make neither the one nor the other, but employs those different artificers. All of them find it in their interest to employ their whole industry in ways in which they have some advantage over their neighbors, and to purchase, with a part of its produce, whatever else they have occasion for. And he infers, that what is prudence in the conduct of every private family, can scarcely be folly in that of a great kingdom.[61]

The world today, no matter how "free" it seems on the surface, is fettered with the very same types of rules, regulations, controls, and commands that classical economists such Nassau Senior spoke out against a century-and-a-half ago. And the advocate of freedom again reminds politicians and the general public that the greater wisdom is to allow each man to have the liberty and discretion to find his own best place in a market system of division of labor, out of which can come far greater wealth and prosperity than any politically controlling hand could ever produce. If this is true, if Adam Smith and others like Nassau Senior were right, then there is no need for or use in allowing the follies of others to delay freedom in the United States. And through freedom in the United States, a new beacon light of liberty for the rest of the world.

Classical Liberalism and a Global Economy of the Future

On January 15, 1846, as the battle for free trade in Great Britain was reaching its conclusion, Richard Cobden spoke before a vast crowd of 9,000 people in Manchester, England. Assuring his listeners that their goal of abolishing protectionism and establishing a regime of free trade was now finally at hand after many years of effort, Cobden at the end of his address chose to reflect on the wider and more far-reaching consequences that he believed were ahead, following the triumph of freedom of trade:

> I can say that I have taken as large and great a view of the effects of this mighty principle [of free trade] as ever did any man who dreamt over it in his own study. . . . I see in the Free Trade principle that which shall act on the moral world as the principle of gravitation in the universe— drawing men together, thrusting aside the antagonism of race, and creed, and language, and uniting us in the bonds of eternal peace. I have looked even further. . . . I believe that the effect will be to change the face of the world. . . . I believe that the desire and the motive for large and mighty empires; for gigantic armies and navies . . . will die away;

I believe such things will cease to be necessary, or to be used, when men become one family, and freely exchanges the fruits of his labor with his brother man.[62]

A dream? Perhaps. But free trade and its classical liberal underpinning did change the world in ways that, while not as fantastic as in Cobden's prevision of the future, were nonetheless momentous, as we have seen. The accomplishment of more of Cobden's dream was cut short by the counter-revolution of collectivism in its socialist, interventionist, and welfare statist forms in the 20th century. The counter-revolution has now petered out. Classical liberal ideas concerning human freedom, the crucial importance of private property, the value of individual self-responsibility, and the need to limit government to a narrow "night-watchman" function are beginning to have a renewed life following the wreckage of statism. And if it is triumphant, the global economy of the 21st century may very well bring with it a world of individual liberty, international peace, and cosmopolitan prosperity. What a reward after the agony of the 20th century, if only we have the understanding and the will to try!

Notes

[1] These statistics are taken from the 1995 and 1996 editions of *The World Almanac and Book of Facts* (Mahwah, NJ: Funk& Wagnalls).

[2] The next several pages on the history of the success of the free trade movement in 19th-century Great Britain draw from Richard M. Ebeling, "Free Trade, Peace and Goodwill Among Nations: The Sesquicentennial of the Triumph of Free Trade," *Freedom Daily* (June 1996): 10-17.

[3] Adam Smith, *An Inquiry into the Nature and Causes of the Wealth of Nations* [1776], Edwin Cannan edition (New York: Modern Library, 1937), 651.

[4] Ibid., 437-38.

[5] See Eli F. Heckscher, *The Continental System: An Economic Interpretation* [1922] (Gloucester, MA: Peter Smith, 1964) for a detailed study of the mercantilist-protectionist polices during the Napoleonic Wars.

[6] Francis W. Hirst, *From Adam Smith to Philip Snowden: A History of Free Trade in Great Britain* (London: T. Fisher Unwin, Ltd., 1925), 13; for histories of the free trade movement in Great Britain, see

Archibald Prentice, *History of the Anti-Corn-Law League* [1853] (New York: Augustus M. Kelley, 1968); Francis W. Hirst, ed., *Free Trade and Other Fundamental Doctrines of the Manchester School* [1903] (New York: Augustus M. Kelley, 1968); George Armitage-Smith, *The Free-Trade Movement and Its Results* [1903] (Freeport, NY: Books for Libraries Press, 1969); John Morley, *The Life of Richard Cobden* (London: T. Fisher Unwin, 1903); and Norman McCord, *The Anti-Corn Law League, 1838-1846* (London: Unwin University Books, 1968). For a history of free trade ideas throughout the ages, see Douglas A. Irwin, *Against the Tide: An Intellectual History of Free Trade* (Princeton, NJ: Princeton University Press, 1996).

[7] Quoted in Francis W. Hirst, *From Adam Smith to Philip Snowden*, 22.

[8] Quoted in J. A. Hobson, *Richard Cobden: The International Man* [1919] (London: Ernest Benn, Ltd., 1968), 41.

[9] Norman McCord, ed. *Free Trade: Theory and Practice from Adam Smith to Keynes* (Newton Abbot, UK: David and Charles, 1970), 91-92.

[10] Charles F. Bastable, *The Commerce of Nations*, 2nd ed. (London: Methuen & Co., 1899); and Gustav Stolper, *This Age of Fable: The Political and Economic World We Live In* (New York: Reynal & Hitchcock, 1942), 7-8.

[11] Wilhelm Röpke, *International Order and Economic Integration* (Dordrecht-Holland: D. Reidel Publishing Co., 1959), 72-79; and Richard M. Ebeling, "World Peace, International Order and Classical Liberalism," *International Journal of World Peace* (December 1995): 47-68.

[12] Oskar Morgenstern, *International Financial Transactions and Business Cycles* (Princeton, NJ: Princeton University Press, 1959), 17, 19, 21; also see John Maynard Keynes, *The Economic Consequences of the Peace* [1919] (New York: Harper & Row, Publishers, 1971), 10-12; Gustav Stolper, *This Age of Fables: The Political and Economic World We Live In* (New York: Reynal & Hitchcock, 1942), 7-9; and Joseph A. Schumpeter, "An Economic Interpretation of Our Time: The Lowell Lectures" [1941] in *The Economics and Sociology of Capitalism* (Princeton, NJ: Princeton University Press, 1991), 339-40.

[13] See Wilhelm Röpke, *German Commercial Policy* (London: Longmans, Green and Co., 1934); Constanino Bresciani-Turroni, " 'Living Space' versus an International System," *Al Qanoun Wal Iqtisad*, Vol. X, No. 1-2 (1940): 35-68; Arcadius Kahan, "Nineteenth-Century European Experience with Policies of Economic Nationalism," in *Economic Nationalism in Old and New States*, ed. Harry G. Johnson (Chicago: University of Chicago Press, 1967), 17-30; and Richard M. Ebeling, "The Political Myths and Economic Realities of the Welfare State" in *American Perestroika: The Demise of the Welfare State*, ed. Richard M. Ebeling, Champions of Freedom Series, Vol. 23 (Hillsdale, MI: Hillsdale College Press, 1995), 3-38.

[14] See Gustav Cassel, *Recent Monopolistic Tendencies in Industry and Trade: Being an Analysis of the Nature and Causes of the Poverty of Nations* (Geneva: League of Nations, 1927); Cassel, "From Protectionism Through Planned Economy to Dictatorship" [Richard Cobden Lecture, 1934], reprinted in *Planned Society: Yesterday, Today and Tomorrow,* ed. Findley MacKenzie (New York: Prentice-Hall, 1937), 775-98; William E. Rappard, "The Common Menace of Economic and Military Armaments" [Richard Cobden Lecture, 1936], reprinted in *Varia Politica: Publies ou Reimprimes a l'occasion du soixante-dixeme anniversaire de William E. Rappard* (Zurich: Editions Polygraphiques, 1953), 76-100; Rappard, "Economic Nationalism," in *Authority and the Individual, Harvard Tercentenary Conference of Arts and Sciences* (Cambridge, MA: Harvard University Press, 1937), 74-112; Rappard, *Post-War Efforts for Freer Trade* (Geneva: Geneva Research Center, 1938); Allen G. B. Fisher, *Economic Self-Sufficiency,* Oxford Pamphlets on World Affairs, No. 4 (Oxford: Clarendon Press, 1939); Michael A. Heilperin, *Studies in Economic Nationalism* (Geneva: Librairie E. Droz, 1962); also Robert Higgs, *Crisis and Leviathan* (Oxford: Oxford University Press, 1987), 123-94; and Robert Nisbet, *The Present Age* (New York: Harper & Row, Publishers, 1988), 1-83.

[15] Moritz J. Bonn, *The World Crisis, and the Teaching of the Manchester School* [The Third Cobden Lecture] (London: Cobden-Sanderson, 1931); Ludwig von Mises, "The Causes of the Economic Crisis" [1931] in *On the Manipulation of Money and Credit* (Dobbs Ferry, NY: Free Market Books, 1978), 173-203; Mises, "The Disintegration of the International Division of Labor," [1938] in *Money, Method and the Market Process: Essays by Ludwig von Mises,* ed. Richard M. Ebeling (Norwell, MA: Kluwer Academic Press, 1990), 113-36; Lionel Robbins, *The Great Depression* (London: Macmillan Co., Ltd., 1934); Robbins, *Economic Planning and Intenational Order* (London: Macmillan Co., 1937); Fritz Machlup, *Führer durch die Krisenpolitik* (Vienna: Julius Springer, 1934); Gottfried Haberler, *Liberale und Planwirtschaft-liche Handelspolitik* (Berlin: Junker und Dunnhaupt, 1934); and Wilhelm Röpke, *International Economic Disintegration* [1942] (Philadelphia: Porcupine Press, 1978).

[16] Benito Mussolini, "The Doctrine of Fascism" [1932] in *Communism, Facism, and Democracy: The Theoretical Foundations,* ed. Carl Cohen (New York: Random House, 1962), 351-52; see also Michael A. Heilperin, "Totalitarian Trade," *World Affairs Interpreter* (January 1941): 1-8.

[17] For a brief summary of the common features of economic policy in Hitler's Nazi Germany and Franklin Roosevelt's America under the first New Deal, see Robert Skidelsky, *The Road from Freedom: The Economic and Political Consequences of the End of Communism* (New York: Allen Lane, Penguin Press, 1996), 60-63.

[18] John Maynard Keynes, *The General Theory of Employment, Interest and Money* [1936] (Cambridge: Macmillan Press, Ltd., 1973), xxvi.

[19] Cf., Ludwig von Mises, "Economic Nationalism and Peaceful Economic Cooperation" [1943] in *Money, Method, and the Market Process: Essays by Ludwig von Mises*, ed. Richard M. Ebeling (Norwell, MA: Kluwer Academic Press, 1990), 158-59.

[20] See Wilhelm Röpke, "The Economics of Full Employment" [1952] in *The Critics of Keynesian Economics*, ed. Henry Hazlitt (Princeton, NJ: D. Van Nostrand, 1960), esp. 381-84; Michael A. Heilperin, *The Trade of Nations*, 2nd ed. (New York: Alfred A. Knopf, 1952), 88-105, 123-33; Heilperin, *Studies in Economic Nationalism*, 97-128; and Henry Hazlitt, *The Failure of the "New Economics": An Analysis of the Keynesian Fallacies* (Princeton, NJ: D. Van Nostrand, 1959), 337-73.

[21] Seymour E. Harris, "International Economics: Introduction" in *The New Economics: Keynes' Influence on Theory and Public Policy*, ed. Seymour E. Harris (New York: Alfred A. Knopf, 1947), 253, 259.

[22] See Melvyn B. Krauss, *The New Protectionism: The Welfare State and International Trade* (New York: New York University Press, 1978), for a detailed and insightful analysis of the incompatibility of an international order of free trade and the intrusive and extensive modern welfare state.

[23] Cf., Norman Angell, *This Have and Have-Not Business: Political Fantasy and Economic Fact* (London: Hamish Hamilton, Publishers, 1936), for a critical study of the errors in the idea that nations can permanently improve their economic well-being by monopolizing control of natural resources at the expense of their potential trading partners. See also Eugene Staley, *Raw Materials in War and Peace* (New York: Council on Foreign Relations, 1937); and Ludwig von Mises, "Der Volkerbund und das Rohstoff Problem" [The League of Nations and the Problem of Raw Materials], *The New Commonwealth Quarterly* (June 1937): 15-25.

[24] Moritz J. Bonn, "International Economic Relations between Governments: A Source of World Peace or Friction?" *Proceedings of the Academy of Political Science* (May 1945): 123.

[25] See Richard M. Ebeling, "World Peace, International Order, and Classical Liberalism," *International Journal of World Peace* (December 1995), esp. 47-54; on the extent and types of government influences on international investment decisions in the pre-World War I period, see Herbert Feis, *Europe: The World's Banker, 1870-1914* [1930] (Clifton, NJ: Augustus M. Kelley, 1974); and Eugene Staley, *War and the Private Investor* [1935] (New York: Herbert Fertig, 1967).

[26] See James G. Smith, *Economic Planning and the Tariff* (Princeton, NJ: Princeton University Press, 1934).

[27] Henry Hazlitt, "The Coming Economic Pattern: Free Trade or State Domination?" *The American Scholar* (Winter 1944-45): 9-10. The difference between the two systems of international economic order was explained by Henry Hazlitt toward the end of the Second World War: "Freedom of trade, in the eyes of Adam Smith and his 19th-century successors in the liberal tradition, meant freedom from government interference.... They wanted a removal of prohibitions and of nearly all tariffs. But they did not ask for positive 'encouragement' or artificial stimulants. They were as much opposed to bounties as they were to barriers. What the older liberals meant by freedom, in short, was the freedom of the individual citizen.... The world barriers to international trade in the 1930s, for which every large nation was in part responsible, but in the erection of which the totalitarian governments went to the greatest lengths, brought about such chaos that few responsible persons now undertake to defend them. High tariffs, import quotas, export subsidies, competitive currency depreciation, blocked currencies, bilateral arrangements, forced barter—all these are today deplored by lip in all respectable circles. The demand now is for International Cooperation. But when the concrete proposals for this international cooperation are examined, it turns out to be something radically different from the international cooperation hoped for by the older liberals. It is not the freedom of the private citizens of any country to trade with the private citizens of any other. It is not primarily the cooperation among private citizens of different countries at all. It is primarily cooperation among governments. As in the thirties, it is governments that are going to take matters in hand. But instead, as in the wicked thirties, of restricting trade and making economic war upon each other, this time, we are told, the governments are going to direct and stimulate trade in the interests of peace. It is a pleasant fantasy; but there are the gravest reasons for doubting that it will ever be realized.... For government officials, even when they really understand (which is very rarely) the basic economic forces they are trying to control, are almost never disinterested. They are almost certain to reflect the special interests of some pressure group. The interests of the pressure groups represented by the bureaucrats of one nation are certain to clash with those of the pressure groups represented by the bureaucrats of another. And these conflicting interests, precisely because they are represented by their representative governments, are far more likely to clash openly, directly and politically than in a world of genuine free trade."

[28] David Osterfeld, "The World Bank and the IMF: Misbegotten Sisters," in *The Collapse of Development Planning*, ed. Peter J. Boettke (New York: New York University Press, 1994), 186.

[29] Gottfried Haberler, "The Liberal International Economic Order in Historical Perspective," in *Challenges to a Liberal International Economic Order*, ed. Ryan C. Amacher, Gottfried Haberler, and Thomas D. Willett (Washington, D.C.: 1979), 49-50; see also Jagdish Bhagwati, *Protectionism* (Cambridge, MA: MIT Press, 1988), 1-15.

[30] Jan Tumlir, *Protectionism: Trade Policy in Democratic Societies* (Washington, D.C.: 1985), 38-39; see also Jan Tumlir, "The New Protectionism, Cartels and the International Order," in *Challenges to a Liberal International Order*, op. cit., 239-58.

[31] "Public choice" theory has cogently shown how the political arena can be understood as a market in which redistributive privileges are given to successful special interest groups that have sufficient incentives to expend scarce resources in the process of political lobbying; at the same time, those holding political office have incentive to "sell" favors, subsidies, and redistributions in exchange for votes and financial contributions; and, as well, those who work in the bureaucracies have incentives to rationalize extensions of government regulation and control to enhance their own power and position in the society. For applications of the public choice approach to the problems of government intervention and management in international trade, commerce, and investment, see Charles K. Rowley, Willem Thorbecke, and Richard E. Wagner, *Trade Protection in the United States* (Brookfield, VT: Edward Elgar, 1995); also Roland Vaubel, "The Political Economy of the IMF: A Public Choice Analysis," in *Perpetuating Poverty: The World Bank, the IMF, and the Developing World*, ed. Doug Bandow and Ian Vasquez (Washington, D.C.: Cato Institute, 1994), 37-55.

[32] The essays in *Perpetuating Poverty*, ibid., document the political philosophy guiding and deleterious consequences following from the policies of the IMF and the World Bank on developing nations around the world. Development economist Peter T. Bauer has for years analyzed the ideas behind and the effects resulting from the programs instituted by these international organizations, as well as various foreign aid programs provided by western governments; see, e.g., his books, *Equality, the Third World and Economic Delusion* (London: Weidenfeld and Nicolson, 1981) and *Reality and Rhetoric: Studies in the Economics of Development* (Cambridge, MA: Harvard University Press, 1984). See also Karl Brunner, ed., *The First and the Third World: Essays on the New International Economic Order* (Rochester, NY: University of Rochester Policy Center Pub-

lications, 1978); Melvyn B. Krauss, *Development Without Aid: Growth, Poverty and Government* (New York: McGraw-Hill, 1983); Deepak Lal, *The Poverty of "Development Economics"* (Cambridge, MA: Harvard University Press, 1985); and Deepak Lal, *The Limits of International Cooperation* (London: Institute of Economic Affairs, 1990). On the World Bank, see Bryan T. Johnson, *The World Bank and Economic Growth: 50 Years of Failure* (Washington, D.C.: Heritage Foundation, 1996), *Backgrounder* No. 1082; and Mark Skousen, "Austrian Capital Theory and Economic Development in the Third World," in *Austrian Economics: Perspectives on the Past and Prospects for the Future,* ed. Richard M. Ebeling, Champions of Freedom Series, Vol. 17 (Hillsdale, MI: Hillsdale College Press, 1991), 355-78.

[33] See James Bovard, *The Fair Trade Fraud* (New York: St. Martin's Press, 1991) for a critical analysis of the notion of "fair trade" instead of free trade and its manipulation to serve the goals of special interest groups.

[34] Friedrich A. Hayek, *Law, Legislation and Liberty,* Vol. II: "The Mirage of Social Justice" (Chicago: University of Chicago Press, 1976).

[35] Jagdish Bhagwati, *The World Trading System at Risk* (Princeton, NJ: Princeton University Press, 1991), 22.

[36] From "About the WTO," "WTO Home Page," www@wto-org.

[37] William Rappard (1883-1958) founded the Graduate Institute of International Studies in Geneva, Switzerland, in 1928. Under his supervision, especially in the years between the two World Wars, the Institute brought together, either as permanent faculty or as visiting professors and lecturers, some of the finest scholars of the times. Among the faculty in the 1930s, for example, were Paul Mantoux, Ludwig von Mises, Wilhelm Röpke, Michael A. Heilperin, Guglielomo Ferrero, Hans Kelsen, and Paul Guggenheim. For a concise appreciation of Rappard's contributions as an economist, political scientist, historian, and world peace advocate, see Albert Picot, *Potrait de William Rappard* (Neuchatel: Editions de la Baconneire, 1963); and for a recent, detailed biography of Rappard's life and work, see Victor Monnier, *William Rappard: Defenseur des libertes, serviteur de son pays et de la communaute internationale* (Geneve: Edition Slatkin, 1995). For an overview of the Institute's work for free trade, democratic government, and world peace during the period that Rappard was the director, see the forty-year anniversary volume, *HEI, 1927-1967* (Geneve: Institut Universitaire de Hautes Etudes Internationales, 1967). It is, perhaps, interesting to note that when Rappard was twenty-five he spent the 1908-1909 semester studying at the University of Vienna with the then leading members of the Austrian School of Economics; see Monnier, *William Rappard,* 40-45.

[38] William E. Rappard, "The Common Menace of Economic and Military Armaments," [1936] reprinted in *Varia Politica* (Zurich: Editions Polygraphiques, 1953), 100.

[39] William E. Rappard, *The Crisis of Democracy* (Chicago: University of Chicago Press, 1938), 267-68.

[40] William E. Rappard, "Economic Nationalism," in *Authority and the Individual: Harvard Tercentenary Conference of Arts and Sciences* (Cambridge, MA: Harvard University Press, 1937), 78, 83-84; see also the valuable essays on this topic in Michael A. Heilperin, *Studies in Economic Nationalism* (Geneva: Librairie E. Droz, 1962).

[41] In fairness, it should be pointed out that in a series of recent speeches, Mr. Renato Ruggiero, Director-General of the WTO, has forcefully argued for what he has called a "borderless world," that would represent "a free global market and a free global trading system." He has warned of the danger "of a power-based system [of] competing [regional trading] blocs" that "attempt to regionalize the global economy," and which would be a threat even to the degree of liberalized world trade that presently exists. As Mr. Ruggiero also has correctly pointed out, "It comes down to a question of the sort of world we want to live in." See his addresses, "Implications for Trade in a Borderless World," delivered to the World Trade Congress, Singapore, 24 April 1996, and "The Road Ahead: International Trade Policy in the Era of the WTO," The Fourth Annual Sylvia Ostry Lecture, Ottawa, Canada, 28 May 1996 (www.wto.org/, press releases 46 & 49). But this is precisely the problem. While the rhetoric used, including Mr. Ruggiero's, resonates with the language of free trade, open markets, and global competition, the reality of the policies advocated and implemented by the member states of the WTO, and the statement of actual principles underlying the purpose of the WTO, are inconsistent with any real depoliticized, privatized system of freedom of trade, commmerce, and investment around the world. The governments of the world do not want free trade; they want managed trade that is "liberal" when and to the extent that it is considered consistent with, or supportive of, their respective interventionist-welfare-statist domestic policies.

[42] Ludwig von Mises, *Liberalism in the Classical Tradition* [1927] (Irvington-on-Hudson, NY: Foundation for Economic Education, 1985), 105-6; and Edwin R. A. Seligman, *Principles of Economics*, 6th ed. (New York: Longmans, Green, and Co., 1914), 569: "The essence of free trade is cosmopolitanism; the essence of protectionism is nationalism."

[43] See Richard M. Ebeling, "The Political Myths and Economic Realities of the Welfare State," in *American Perestroika: The Demise of the Welfare State*, Champions of Freedom Series, Vol. 23 (Hillsdale, MI: Hillsdale College Press, 1995), 3-38.

[44] Cf., Paul Craig Roberts and Lawrence M. Stratton, *The New Color Line: How Quotas and Privileges Destroy Democracy* (Washington, D.C.: Regnery Publishing, Inc., 1995), iii, 165: "Critical Race Theory and radical feminism are Marxist to the core. [Critical Race Theorists] see American democracy as an unjust combination by whites to oppress blacks. Feminism applies the same denial of goodwill to the genders. . . . The determinism of the new Marxism allows whites no more escape from their racial consciousness than the old Marxism allowed the bourgeoisie to transcend their class consciousness." Also Richard M. Ebeling, "Collectivist Myths and Racial Prejudices," *Freedom Daily* (October 1991): 6-10; reprinted in *Individualism, Civil Liberties, and the State*, ed. Jacob G. Hornberger and Richard M. Ebeling (Fairfax, VA: Future of Freedom Foundation, 1997).

[45] Ludwig von Mises, *Omnipotent Government: The Rise of the Total State and Total War* (New Haven: Yale University Press, 1944), 91-92; *Liberalism in the Classical Tradition*, op. cit., 112-13.

[46] See Richard M. Ebeling, "Liberalism and Collectivism in the 20th Century," in *The End of "Isms"? Reflections on the Fate of Ideological Politics After Communism's Collapse*, ed. Alexsandras Shtromas (New York: Blackwell Publishers, 1994), 69-84.

[47] Frederic Bastiat, "The Law" in *Selected Essays on Political Economy* (Princeton, NJ: D. Van Nostrand Co., Inc., 1964), 51-96.

[48] Histories of the private sector's successful handling of "social services" in the past in America and Great Britain have begun to appear, most notably, Marvin Olasky, *The Tragedy of American Compassion* (Washington, D.C.: Regnery Gateway, 1992); and David Green, *Reinventing Civil Society: The Rediscovery of Welfare Without Politics* (London: Institute of Economic Affairs, 1993); also Robert Whalen, *The Corrosion of Charity: From Moral Renewal to the Contract Culture* (London: Institute of Economic Affairs, 1996).

[49] Wilhelm Röpke, *Welfare, Freedom, and Inflation* (Auburn, AL: University of Alabama Press, 1964), 29.

[50] See Richard M. Ebeling, "How Economics Became the Dismal Science," in *Economic Education: What Should We Learn About the Free Market?* ed. Richard M. Ebeling, Champions of Freedom Series, Vol. 22 (Hillsdale, MI: Hillsdale College Press, 1994), 51-83; also, Richard M. Ebeling, "Free Trade, Managed Trade and the State," in *The Case for Free Trade and Open Immigration*, ed. Richard M. Ebeling and Jacob G. Hornberger (Fairfax, VA: Future of Freedom Foundation, 1995), 2-29.

[51] Public choice theory, as pointed out in note 31, has insightfully demonstrated the nature and workings of special-interest politics in democratic society; see James M. Buchanan, Robert D. Tollison, and Gordon Tullock, eds., *Toward a Theory of the Rent-Seeking Society*

(College Station, TX: Texas A&M University Press, 1980); Robert E. McCormick and Robert D. Tollison, *Politicians, Legislation, and the Economy: An Inquiry into the Interest-Group Theory of Government* (Boston: Martinus Nijhoff Publishing, 1981); Gordon Tullock, *The Economics of Special Privilege and Rent Seeking* (Boston: Kluwer Academic Publishers, 1989); and Fred S. McChesney and William F. Shughart, eds., *The Causes and Consequences of Antitrust: A Public Choice Perspective* (Chicago: University of Chicago Press, 1995).

[52] See Israel M. Kirzner, "The Perils of Regulation: A Market-Process Approach," in *Discovery and the Capitalist Process* (Chicago: University of Chicago Press, 1985), 199-249, also reprinted in *Austrian Economics: A Reader*, ed. Richard M. Ebeling, Champions of Freedom Series, Vol. 18 (Hillsdale, MI: Hillsdale College Press, 1991), 618-55; and Dominick T. Armentano, *Antitrust and Monopoly: Anatomy of a Policy Failure* (New York: John Wiley and Sons, 1982); and D. T. Armentano, *Antitrust Policy: The Case for Repeal* (Washington, D.C.: Cato Institute, 1985); S. C. Littlechild, *The Fallacy of the Mixed Economy: An Austrian Critique of Economic Theory and Policy* (London: Institute of Economic Affairs, 1978); also Robert W. Poole, ed., *Instead of Regulation: Alternatives to Federal Regulatory Agencies* (Lexington, MA: Lexington Books, 1982)

[53] Ludwig von Mises, "Autarky and Its Consequences," [1943] in *Money, Method, and the Market Process: Essays by Ludwig von Mises*, ed. Richard M. Ebeling (Norwell, MA: Kluwer Academic Publishers, 1990), 145.

[54] Melchior Palyi, *The Twilight of Gold, 1914-1936: Myths and Realities* (Chicago: Henry Regnery Co., 1972), 5, 9; see also Wilhelm Röpke, *International Order and Economic Integration* (Dordrecht, Holland: D. Reidel Publishing Co., 1959), 75-77.

[55] On the monetary mismanagement of Great Britain, France, Germany, and the United States during World War I, see J. Laurence Laughlin, *A New Exposition of Money, Credit, and Prices*, Vol. II (Chicago: University of Chicago Press, 1931), 515-626; Edwin W. Kemmerer, *Money: The Principles of Money and Their Exemplification in Outstanding Chapters of Monetary History* (New York: Macmillan Co., 1935), 271-318; on the period leading up and during the Great Depression, see Friedrich A. Hayek, "The Fate of the Gold Standard," [1932] in *Money, Capital, and Fluctuations: Early Essays* (Chicago: University of Chicago Press, 1984), 118-35; Lionel Robbins, *The Great Depression* (New York: Macmillan Co., 1934); Frederic Benham, *British Monetary Policy* (London: P. S. King and Son, Ltd., 1932); H. F. Fraser, *Great Britain and the Gold Standard* (New York: Macmillan Co., 1933); C. A. Phillips, T. F. McManus, and R. W. Nelson, *Banking and the Business Cycle* (New York: Macmillan Co., 1937); and Melchior Palyi, *The Twilight of Gold*, op. cit.

[56] Moritz J. Bonn, "The Gold Standard in International Relations," in *Problems of Peace*, 8th Series, ed. William E. Rappard [1934] (Freeport, NY: Books for Libraries Press, 1968), 163-79; and T. E. Gregory, *The Gold Standard and Its Future*, 3rd ed. (New York: E. P. Dutton & Co., Inc., 1935), 1-29.

[57] See Friedrich A. Hayek, *Monetary Nationalism, and International Stability* [1937] (New York: Augustus M. Kelley, 1971); Lionel Robbins, *Economic Planning and International Order* (New York: Macmillan Co., 1937), 280-301; Michael A. Heilperin, *International Monetary Economics* (London: Longmans, Green and Co., 1939); and Michael A. Heilperin, *Aspects of the Pathology of Money: Monetary Essays from Four Decades* (London: Michael Joseph, 1968).

[58] The case has been made, e.g., by Richard B. McKenzie and Dwight R. Lee, *Quicksilver Capital: How the Rapid Movement of Wealth Has Changed the World* (New York: Free Press, 1991), that the recent development of computerized global capital markets have served to introduce a new external check on discretionary monetary and fiscal policies by national governments, because any adverse economic policy anticipated or introduced in a particular country immediately results in financial capital fleeing from that nation into alternative markets around the world—at the mere pressing of a computer key. Computer technology and the integration of global financial markets certainly do provide financial capital investors greater and quicker mobility. But while the "corridor" of national governmental discretion may have been narrowed due to these market developments, this still has not eliminated the power or the domestic policy interests of governments in attempting to manipulate domestic interest rates, foreign exchange rates, and the general level of prices and wages in their respective countries. The policymakers now must merely more carefully weigh the costs of (perhaps significant) marginal capital outflows and their impacts on interests rates, the foreign exchange, and the availability of loanable funds for both government and private sector borrowing in comparison to the domestic political benefits from implementing the particular policy in question. Furthermore, while financial capital can take "flight" in the face of expected or actual "negative" policies, real capital (physical plant and equipment) and the labor force cannot. Those buying the financial assets being sold by those who wish to take their "quicksilver capital" and flee will view the purchase of titles to the real capital up for sale as bargains (at least in the short run); after all, those desiring to flee can only do so if they find a willing buyer, and that will be a function of the price at which those wishing to flee are willing to sell.

59 On the possibilities and workability of a market-generated monetary order and system of free banking, see Ludwig von Mises,
"Monetary Stabilization and Cyclical Policy," [1928] in *On the Manipulation of Money and Credit* (Dobbs Ferry, NY: Free Market Books,
1978), 138-40; Ludwig von Mises, *Human Action, A Treatise on Eco-
nomics*, 3rd ed. rev. (Chicago: Henry Regnery Co., 1966), 440-48;
Ludwig von Mises, *The Theory of Money and Credit*, 3rd ed. rev. (In-
dianapolis: Liberty Classics, [1953] 1981), 434-38; Richard M. Ebeling,
"Ludwig von Mises and the Gold Standard," in *The Gold Standard:
An Austrian Perspective*, ed. Llewellyn H. Rockwell (Lexington, MA:
Lexington Books, 1985), 35-59; Lawrence H. White, "Mises on Free
Banking and Fractional Reserves," in *A Man of Principle: Essays in
Honor of Hans F. Sennholz*, ed. John W. Robbins and Mark Spangler
(Grove City, PA: Grove City College Press), 517-33; Vera C. Smith,
The Rationale of Central Banking and the Free Banking Alternative
[1936] (Indianapolis: Liberty Press, 1990); Friedrich A. Hayek,
"Denationalization of Money—the Argument Refined," [1978] in
Economic Freedom (New York: Blackwell Publishers, 1991), 125-235;
Lawrence H. White, *Free Banking in Britain: Theory, Experience, and
Debate, 1800-1845* (Cambridge, MA: Cambridge University Press,
1984); Lawrence H. White, *Competition and Currency: Essays on Free
Banking and Money* (New York: New York University Press, 1989);
George A. Selgin, *The Theory of Free Banking: Money Supply Under
Competitive Note Issue* (Totowa, NJ: Rowman & Littlefield, Publish-
ers, 1988); Hans Sennholz, *Money and Freedom* (Cedar Falls, IA: Center
for Futures Education, Inc., 1985); Kevin Dowd, *Private Money: The
Path to Monetary Stability* (London: Institute of Economic Affairs,
1988); Kevin Dowd, *The State and the Monetary System* (New York:
St. Martin's Press, 1989); Kevin Dowd, *Laissez Faire Banking* (New
York: Routledge, 1993); Kevin Dowd, ed., *The Experience of Free Banking* (New York: Routledge, 1992); Steven Horwitz, *Monetary Evolution, Free Banking and Economic Order* (Boulder, CO: Westview Press,
1992); Murray N. Rothbard, *The Case for a 100 Percent Gold Dollar*
[1962] (Auburn, AL: Ludwig von Mises Institute, 1991); and Mark
Skousen, *Economics of a Pure Gold Standard* (Auburn, AL: Ludwig
von Mises Institute, 1988).

60 Henry Dunning MacLeod, *The History of Economics* (London: Bliss, Sands
and Co., 1896), 82, 84 (italics in original); also see Henry Fawcett, *Manual
of Political Economy*, 4th ed. (London: Macmillan and Co., 1874), 389-90.

61 Nassau Senior, *Industrial Efficiency and Social Economy*, Vol. II (New
York: Henry Holt and Co., 1928), 159, 193.

62 Francis W. Hirst, ed., *Free Trade and Other Fundamental Doctrines of the
Manchester School* [1903] (New York: Augustus M. Kelley, 1968), 229.

CHARLES D. VAN EATON

Will Capitalism Survive?

More than fifty years ago, in his famous book *Capitalism, Socialism, and Democracy,* the great Harvard economist Joseph A. Schumpeter wrote that capitalism was an "engine of mass production, which unavoidably means also production for the masses."[1] He went on to add:

> It is the cheap cloth, the cheap cotton and rayon fabric, boots, motorcars, and so on that are the typical achievements of capitalist production, and not, as a rule, improvements that would mean as much to the rich man. Queen Elizabeth owned silk stockings. The capitalist achievement does not typically consist of providing silk stockings for queens but in bringing them within reach of factory girls in return for steadily decreasing amounts of effort.[2]

Schumpeter was no socialist. Indeed, he was not even a mild supporter of the New Deal, which was the great liberal experiment of his era. He opposed government intervention in the economy because, he said, it "fetters" capitalism and makes it less productive. It also hurts those it is supposedly designed to help: the poor and the members of the working class. They are the ones most dependent on a dynamic, market-driven, job-creating economy.

Destroying the Foundations of Capitalism

But in 1942 when Schumpeter asked "Will capitalism survive?", his answer was "No." Certainly he was an ardent defender of capitalism. He genuinely believed that the free market is the most effective provider of goods and services. But he argued that capitalism's very success in delivering the masses from grinding poverty works inexorably to destroy the moral and cultural foundations on which it rests.

In the prologue to *Capitalism, Socialism, and Democracy,* Schumpeter noted:

> The thesis I shall endeavor to establish is that the actual and perspective performance of the capitalist system is such as to negate the idea of its breaking down under the weight of economic failure. Rather, its very success undermines the social institutions which protect it and inevitably creates the conditions in which it will not be able to live. The end result of this is that its success will strongly point to socialism (or something closely kin to socialism) as its heir apparent.[3]

In Schumpeter's view, the self-destructive nature of capitalism follows from its "anti-heroic" character: "The capitalist process rationalizes behavior and ideas and thereby chases from our minds not only metaphysical belief, but also mystic and romantic ideas of all sorts.... The stock exchange is a poor substitute for the Holy Grail." It also leaves a spiritual void which liberated social critics will try to fill. These critics—educated and subsidized from the economic surplus created by capitalism—have a vested interest in social unrest. Uninterested as they often are in politics and ideology, capitalists stand defenseless before the critics and, sooner or later, they will be vanquished. Even if capitalists are allowed to own and use their property, constraints will be imposed on their actions to make them instruments of those who hate capitalism for its very success.

Not surprisingly, Schumpeter's prophecy has generated a vast literature over the last half-century. In 1981, Arnold Heertje released *Schumpeter's Vision: Capitalism, Socialism, and Democracy after Forty Years*. This book contains eleven essays written by prominent economists and sociologists who, without exception, conclude that Schumpeter was wrong. Capitalism, they contend, will not fail nor will socialism triumph. Why? Because they need each other. Socialist countries fail to produce goods and services efficiently, so they need at least a small dose of capitalism. Likewise, capitalist countries need government intervention in order to manage their economic affairs and to rescue capitalism from self-destruction.

The view of these scholars—that capitalism and socialism are somehow mutually dependent—is a common one, but it only confirms Schumpeter's original argument. In applauding "rescue intervention" to "save" capitalism, it condones the very "fettering" process that Schumpeter saw as the first step on the road to the unfree, unproductive society. It is also a view that is oblivious to history for it regards wealth not as the product of an economic system based on reasonably well-defined private property rights and freedom of exchange, but as something that just exists in the eternal and natural order of things.

Advocates of Socialism on the Right and the Left

Schumpeter's concern about the future of capitalism still bears serious consideration as we address the future of American business. When writing in the late 1930s to early 1940s, Schumpeter thought that capitalism as he knew it might last a hundred more years. We are only a little more than halfway down that road. Thus, the issue is still very much with us.

In context, note the rhetoric of the current presidential campaigns. Recall the buzzwords our current president used four years ago when he ran for and won election to the White

House. Then and now, the air is full of speeches about how we need to use government—directly or indirectly through the tax system—to "right" all kinds of "wrongs" generated by the market process.

In 1992, Mr. Clinton also talked about an economy that was allegedly declining. He called it "the worst economy in the past 50 years." And he entered office with the goal of "stimulating" and "investing in" the economy. He wanted us to "contribute" with higher taxes. Today, he is using the same language in his re-election bid (without, of course, the part about the economy being in such awful shape). At the same time, Republican front-runner Senator Robert Dole has been saying (with utmost sincerity and, of course, with a straight face) something like this: "Corporate profits are at an all-time high while wages and job security are at an all-time low."

If nothing else, such rhetoric from leading members of both major political parties confirms Schumpeter's worst fears. Capitalism, we are being told, is inherently flawed and cannot survive without a healthy dose of government intervention—which is to say, without a healthy dose of socialism-by-another-name in a more subtle and, therefore, more dangerous form.

"Well," you might say, "this is just politics and politicians merely say what they think will get them elected." But politicians are not fools. They say these things because they suspect that, down deep, people really dislike and distrust capitalism, no matter how much they may like or trust what it brings to their table. They have no real understanding of what it is or of how markets operate. The political class knows how to exploit such ignorance—and far too many people don't mind being exploited.

How else can one understand the rhetoric of Pat Buchanan and Richard Gephardt? We know what these men say they want for America: They want "free and fair" trade. But, in reality, they want to put America behind protective walls—away from the forces of world commerce. Now, people often say that things are different in the 1990s because we live in a "world economy." In fact, we have always lived in a world economy. Just recall the biblical story of Joseph. His brothers, driven by envy, plot to kill him. Then they decide to sell him to a band of traders that is traveling to Egypt with goods to sell. *Goods to sell? To Egypt?* Even in ancient times international trade existed on a grand scale.

Mr. Buchanan has aligned himself with "national interest" groups on the right and with American textile companies, which stand to gain billions of dollars at the expense of America's poorest consumers if they get what he says he wants for America. Representative Gephardt promotes the traditional agenda of the left, which is to say that he advocates using the federal government's taxing and spending powers to force businesses to follow a federally prescribed "code of conduct" on trade as well as on wages, pensions, and other so-called "guarantees" to workers and consumers as defined by Washington. Corporate taxes would be changed. Businesses that do what Gephardt wants would see their taxes reduced. Those that do not would see their taxes raised.

According to both Buchanan and Gephardt, then, capitalism isn't good enough, and competition is dangerous. We need an economic system managed from the center. Americans must be compelled by law to bend in service—all in the name of the common good. In more honest times we called this view socialism or, more precisely, fascism. Now, most of us haven't the courage even to give it a name.

Fear of Freedom

The Buchanans and the Gephardts succeed because there is a madness loose in this country—a madness that flows from fear: fear of freedom and the burden of personal responsibility which freedom imposes on every individual.

Author and historian Paul Johnson notes that "seen against the grand perspective of history, capitalism is a relative newcomer."[4] He defines capitalism as "large-scale industrial capitalism in which privately financed, publicly owned corporations, operating in a free market environment, constitute the core of the national economy."[5] By his definition, capitalism is only a little over two hundred years old; as a widely spread process of economic organization, it is barely one hundred years old.

Capitalism's record, judged in terms of its capacity to produce and distribute wealth, is without parallel in human history. Judged also by how well is has operated to serve the poor, Johnson makes the following comment about its early impact on society in England:

> From the very start, industrial capitalism won the approval of the masses. They could not vote in the ballot box, but they voted in a far more impressive manner: with their feet. The poorest members of society value political freedom as much as the richest. But the freedom they value most of all is the freedom to sell their labor and skills in the open market. It was precisely this that industrial capitalism gave to the poorest in society for the first time in human history.... The factory system, however harsh it may now seem to modern eyes, was the road to freedom for millions of agricultural workers. Not only did it offer them an escape from a form of poverty which was grinding and unremitting compared to what could be had in the growing industrial cities, it gave them something they did not have—the ability to move from status to contract, from a stationary place in a static society, with tied cottages and semi-conscript labor, to a mobile place in a dynamic society.[6]

But Johnson, as Schumpeter before him, concludes that the free enterprise idea is losing the intellectual and moral battle. Three of the causes he cites are:

1. the failure of the educational system;
2. the "ecological panic"; and,
3. the growth of government.

The Failure of the Educational System

Our public education system has failed to teach three very important things: reading, writing, and arithmetic. Recently, a story appeared in the *Detroit Free Press* detailing the difficulty many Michigan manufacturers are having finding qualified employees. Now we are told, and it is true, that people really want to work. But these firms are finding it hard to fill two thousand jobs. They have interviewed thousands of people, but to no avail. What did they tell the *Free Press* they needed? People who could read and perform arithmetic at the eighth-grade level.

The "Ecological Panic"

The world is not coming to an end. We are not being killed by environmental poison. We are not about to drown in our garbage. We are not running out of places to put our garbage either. A study done by the EPA notes that at current rates of waste disposal a space equal to one square mile could accommodate a soundly designed landfill holding all of America's waste in a perfectly sealed cell for the next one thousand years.[7] But we are told we must mandate recycling, even though for almost all the things we are often compelled to "recycle," we waste more scarce resources in the "recycling" process than we save.

The Growth of Government

Despite all the plans to balance the federal budget in seven years, the level of government spending relative to Gross Domestic Product will still continue to rise. Indeed, just for the category of federal spending we call "entitlements," by the year 2020, if not before, federal spending will outstrip projected revenues.

A Deeper Malady

But, despite all the forces Johnson ably identifies as threats to the future of capitalism and American business, I feel even he has missed the key point. These forces are less the cause of capitalism's weakness than they are symptoms of a deeper malady. Recall his observations: "The factory system was the road to freedom for millions of agricultural workers." And, "it allowed them to move from status to contract, from a stationary place in a static society . . . to a mobile place in a dynamic society."

These observations are no less true today than they were in the era he was describing, the Industrial Revolution. Now as then, modern capitalism (which by Johnson's preferred definition was nothing more than the joining of new technologies in energy and machine design with an economic system based on freedom of exchange) shatters status and adds a broad range of freedom to new peoples both here and in other places. And this freedom continues to bring the heavy burden of responsibility and—all so frightening because the two are inexorably linked—the stark reality of potential failure.

Socialists of all stripes have never posed themselves as enemies of freedom. On the contrary, they like to argue that they alone really understand what freedom is. But by freedom they most often mean the power—indeed, the entitled right—to actually possess whatever it is that they want. They argue that the kind of freedom that follows from capitalism is negative—freedom from constraint or coercion. This is not real freedom at all in their view.

Socialists contend that is useless to be told that no one is preventing you from trying to attain your economic goals when you lack the power to get what you want right now. If the open competitive market process fails to give you what you want when you want, you are not free. You are a slave. In this context, you have the right to use the state to give you what the market does not. When, and only when, the state is empowered to give you what you want are you truly free.

This, then, is the siren song of socialism: the removal of the prospect of failure. And it has always had a powerful seductive appeal. In times past there have been countless rallies to ban this-or-that and people carrying banners that say, in essence, "Fund Human Needs." Those who are attracted to such slogans think that it is right to use the power of the state to satisfy what they define as "human needs." They succumb to one of the oldest and most dangerous of fallacies.

It is at least as old as the story of the Exodus. Recall the children of Israel. Moses had just led them out of Egyptian bondage. They were on the road to freedom under God, going to a land God had promised them. But the road was long and hard. For the first time in four hundred years the Israelites were free. But as soon as the stark reality of freedom's meaning hit them, they lamented:

> What have you done to us in bringing us out of Egypt?
> ... [F]or it would have been better for us to serve the Egyptians than to die in the wilderness (Exodus 14:11-12).

> And the whole congregation of the people of Israel murmured against Moses and Aaron in the wilderness, and said to them, "would that we had died by the hand of the Lord in the land of Egypt, when we sat by the fleshpots and ate bread to the full; for you have brought us out into this wilderness to kill this whole assembly with hunger" (Exodus 16:2-3).

The freedom that comes with capitalism is—let us admit it—the freedom of the wilderness. It does not guarantee—indeed, it *cannot* guarantee—anything except the right to try, the right to pursue one's dreams.

The Right to Try

The right to try, and only the right to try, is a frightening prospect. As University of California political scientist Paul Seabury reminds us, the only economic system that has brought

so many people so much real wealth also destroys a vision with
which so many people are taken—the vision of a life that is
"both dependable and dependent."

> The medieval system that capitalism supplanted at least
> offered certainty—the certainty of a heritable status. In
> such a setting, there was a form of community that could
> be expected to last. And with this certainty of an un-
> changed community there was also the absence of the
> kinds of anxieties that always attend the exercise of free
> choice and free movement.[8]

Capitalism offers a different kind of community—a "community of competition and strivers." Moreover, it is a kind
of community of competition and strivers that knows no race,
color, nationality, or creed.

So, I come back to where I began. Freedom lays a heavy
burden, and many of us do not really want to bear this burden. In return for security—as if in this world of scarcity such
could ever be had—we are willing to sacrifice some freedom.
But the problem with being willing to sacrifice some freedom is that we have to sacrifice it to someone or something.
And as we have learned from "public choice" theory, that someone or something will seldom give it back because the power
that goes with the managing of other people's lives can pay
handsome rewards.

There is nothing novel in what I have said here. What *is*
novel is the notion, quite recent in American history, that
government is absolutely obliged to intervene at any and every
point in the market process to thwart what flows from "a
community of competition and strivers" and to block, if not
totally eliminate, the "anxieties which attend the free exercise of choice and movement."

And government, with our support far more often than we
would freely admit, has been busy doing just that. At first this
process of using the power of government to replace some

freedom with some security (or at least, the vague promise of security) was slow. The expansion of the government during the New Deal represents an excellent example. Only two of Franklin D. Roosevelt's famous "Four Freedoms" were of the socialist genre: freedom from fear (i.e., economic fear) and freedom from want. But once the politicians caught on to how this sounded to the ear seeking security, there was no turning back. The entire process that started in the 1930s and 1940s has grown to become what sociologist Daniel Bell long ago called the "sense of rising entitlements."

A Sense of Rising Entitlements

We live now in a nation that is trying to find its soul. We all know that socialism of the old textbook variety can't work, but we aren't willing to acknowledge that socialism of the newer and more subtle variety cannot work either. We live in a nation in which the sense of rising entitlements has corrupted the entire political process. What *Public Interest* founding editor Irving Kristol calls the "iron triangle" of the media, the politicians, and the new class of intellectuals who design, administer, and live off of the new programs they have helped to design, stand ready to attack anyone who calls into question the fundamental premises on which they operate. They will not tolerate anyone who will challenge the assumption that government has a moral obligation to eliminate the "anxieties which attend the exercise of free choice and free movement."

Restoring Freedom and Responsibility

In the face of this attack, many are afraid to speak. And no one has shown more cowardice than American businessmen, as Paul Weaver documents in his gripping account, *The*

Suicidal Corporation: How Big Business Fails America. In some part, this is because the pervasive growth of government intervention and the modern welfare state has not been a product of what Nobel laureate F. A. Hayek called the "system of spontaneous order." Rather, it has been growth in the intervention of government and the decay of freedom by invitation. Every request for a tariff, a quota, or state-mandated licensing of one occupation after another has come not from consumers, but from business leaders (not all business leaders, of course, but from a significant number). What they seek is not freedom for all but security for their own interests. The freedom they want is freedom from the pain and uncertainty of competition.

When American automobile firms seek restrictions on imports, they are exercising their own "sense of rising entitlements." When the American textile industry supports the protectionist views of Pat Buchanan or Richard Gephardt, they know what they are doing—they are seeking a governmental shield from the world of "competition and strivers." When the American steel industry asks for—and gets—restrictions on steel imports, they are seeking relief from the "anxieties which attend the exercise of freedom choice." When farmers press for crop subsidies they are doing the same thing. In this setting, we should not be surprised to hear the "little man" request help from government to arrest the vicissitudes of life.

Businessmen, by virtue of their special role in the market economy, should understand how the market system has to work to do what it does best for the great mass of people. But more and more of them are seeking relief from the system. As Schumpeter feared, perhaps the moral foundations of capitalism have been broken beyond repair.

Can capitalism survive? Is there a future for American business? No, not as long as the freedom and personal responsibility on which it depends continue to be attacked from within by capitalists themselves. Only when the American business community begins to refuse alms will the system be saved.

Notes

[1] Joseph Schumpeter, *Capitalism, Socialism, and Democracy* (New York: Harper & Row, 1942; Colophon edition, 1975), 72.
[2] Ibid.
[3] Ibid., 61.
[4] Paul Johnson, "Has Capitalism a Future?," in *Will Capitalism Survive?* (Washington, D.C.: Ethics and Public Policy Center, 1979), 3.
[5] Ibid.
[6] Ibid., 6.
[7] A. Clark Wiseman, "Resources for the Future," cited in Lynn Scarlett, "Integrated Waste Management: Rethinking Solid Waste," in *Policy Insight* (Los Angeles, CA: Reason Foundation, 1991), 9.
[8] Paul Seabury, "The Exquisitely Sensitive Market," in Paul Johnson, op. cit., 25.

CHARLES KOCH

Market-Based Values and the Future of American Business

The shelves of most bookstores are crowded with best-selling business books, but business owners should not limit their reading to just them. They ought to be studying the classic works of Austrian School economist Ludwig von Mises. Mises championed the principles of free enterprise, and he was one of principal sources of the ideas that changed the course of my life and that led to the development of Market-Based Management®, the framework that I credit with the enormous success of Koch Industries.

Market-Based Management® is based on four main assumptions. The first assumption is that today's world is characterized by an unprecedented rate of change—change driven by an accelerating accumulation of knowledge. The second assumption is that prospering in this environment requires a well-founded and internally consistent framework that enables us to interpret and apply new knowledge. The third assumption is that from both theory and history we know that the best framework for dealing with rapid change, especially knowledge-driven change, is one based on economic freedom. The fourth assumption is that this framework should also have five key dimensions: vision, values, incentives, decision rights, and knowledge systems.

Rapid Change

Let us begin by exploring in more detail the one thing, in addition to death and taxes, we can always count on: *change.* There is more change in one year today than there was in a hundred years several centuries ago. What is creating such rapid change? It is primarily an "information revolution" in the knowledge and communications industries. Computers, satellites, e-mail, voice mail, and faxes give us access to more information, and at a faster rate, than anyone ever dreamed possible. Consumers are better informed and have more choices. Manufacturers and suppliers are able to get new products and new services on the market more efficiently and with greater speed. And everyone—from purchasers to business owners and vendors to investors—are able to learn about price changes almost instantly.

These developments are causing a fundamental restructuring of the economy and are forcing companies to change the way they do business in order to survive. Those that constantly adapt to change tend to build more knowledge into their products—products ranging from self-diagnosing machines to genetically engineered grain to performance asphalt. Meanwhile, those companies that haven't adapted to change are being devastated by billion-dollar losses and massive layoffs. Even corporate giants such as GM, IBM, Sears, and, more recently, AT&T, are being forced to make themselves over.

In energy, which is the primary although not exclusive field in which Koch Industries operates, we have seen companies that have been facing equivalent problems. But doomsday predictions that the world would soon run out of hydrocarbons have repeatedly proved false. Over the last fifty years, the remaining years of energy reserves have more than doubled.

Due to continuous technological improvements, oil and gas exploration and development costs continue to fall, increasing supply and lowering prices. In fact, over the last seventy-five years, the price of gasoline, the principal oil product, has fallen in half in constant (before tax) dollars. The same trend holds true for almost every other commodity, from metals to cotton to chickens—all contributing to a dramatic improvement in the standard of living for all.

The Essentials of Market-Based Management®

So how do businesses learn to survive and prosper in this world of accelerating change and increasing complexity? First, it requires them to do more than simply react to change. Businesses must become "change leaders," generating knowledge by creating systems that draw and integrate knowledge from customers, suppliers, competitors, and every part of the firm. And then they must apply this knowledge in a way that adds new value for their customers.

This, in turn, requires more than simply meeting customer expectations—after all, old IBM mainframe computers met customer expectations. It requires a creative process to identify needs that customers haven't even conceived of yet. It requires restructuring the way value is created and delivered. It requires that products, companies, and entire industries be continually redefined and restructured.

Most of all, it requires businesses to develop a complete, integrated framework that is philosophically sound and internally consistent. Merely applying the latest trend, such as "Total Quality Management" or "re-engineering," is not sufficient. No matter how useful these tools may be in solving specific problems, they are not complete systems and they cannot bring about the fundamental changes required. At Koch Industries, we have found that Market-Based Management® does satisfy these requirements of completeness, soundness, and consistency. We believe that it derives its power from theoretical, historical, and practical lessons on what creates prosperity and progress.

Internalizing Free Market Concepts

So how do we apply Market-Based Management® to get results? The first step is getting our employees to internalize certain basic concepts of free market economics. This means going beyond conceptual understanding—beyond being able to pass a test on the concepts—to being skilled in practicing and to be willing to change old habits and old ways of thinking. It also means that employees must continually redefine their roles in their own organization.

Briefly, here are some of the free market concepts that are most important for our employees to internalize:

- Human action, especially human action in the marketplace, is most often based on considerations of subjective value, marginal utility, opportunity cost, comparative advantage, time preference, change, uncertainty, the nature and use of knowledge, and property rights.

- Complex systems, whether societies or businesses, can only function properly through spontaneous order rather than central control.

- The free market—the purest form of spontaneous order—is a discovery process for continually finding better ways to satisfy people's needs.

- Freely adjusting prices and profits and losses are critical mechanisms in this discovery process.

- For a business to succeed, it must identify the needs that it can best satisfy and build the capabilities that will enable it do so.

- Just as in society, the creation and transmission of knowledge within a business require an open marketplace of ideas and profit signals that help employees see what creates value and what doesn't.

• An employee is to a firm as an entrepreneur is to society. In other words, each employee has the same opportunity and obligation to create value in the firm that the firm does in society.

Changing Our Vision

Once these concepts are internalized, we may work on the first key dimension of Market-Based Management®: changing our vision of our businesses and our jobs. Our vision controls the way we think and, therefore, the way we act. If we try to apply Market-Based Management® without changing our vision and without acquiring sound economic principles, we end up doing the same old things in a different way with a different language. We change the form but not the substance. And when that happens, we don't get results.

But when we actually change our vision, we typically get remarkable results. Major improvement or growth in any of Koch Industries' businesses has always been preceded by a change in vision. The same is true for the vision our employees have of their jobs. An example—one repeated many times over—involves an employee whose job was operating one of the process units at a refinery. In the past, his job primarily consisted of following detailed instructions, such as: "Turn the valve when the pressure reaches a certain level." Once the vision of his job was changed from following instructions to optimizing his unit, and he was given the information and the freedom to do so, the employee improved the performance of his unit by *over 20 percent*. Clearly, the vision we have of our jobs determines what we do and the opportunities we see or don't see.

Too often, our vision tends to limit our ability to deal with change and make discoveries because it is formed by old habits, old practices, and old technologies. Thus, when a new technology appears, rather than being used to create a new vision, it tends to be used only to improve the performance of old practices. This can lead to disaster. By the time of the Civil War, for example, weapons had become faster and more accurate. But, even up to World War I, a favorite tactic of military leaders continued to be the massed charge, which increasingly led to wholesale slaughter. The generals' vision of tactics was formed by old practices. They had new technology, but they failed to develop a new vision based on that technology.

The same is true in business. Sears lost out to Wal-Mart in part because Wal-Mart adopted a new vision and Sears didn't. Using developments in information technology, Wal-Mart created an entirely new approach to purchasing and inventory while Sears simply automated its old inventory control system. With its new vision, Wal-Mart was able to cut inventory in half while providing superior customer service. Similarly, the American steel industry was dying until technology was used to rethink the business. This change in vision gave birth to the "mini-mill" and the world's lowest-cost, highest-quality steel. Following the pattern of other industries, companies that clung to the old vision of steel making fell even further behind.

So, in the first key dimension of Market-Based Management®, we must constantly strive to create a new vision for our businesses based on changes in technology and the marketplace. For example, in Koch Industries' beef business we are working to create an information network that will better connect each segment of the "value chain" with what the consumer values. Information on the performance of each animal will guide how cattle are bred, fed, prepared, and packaged to give consumers the products, services, and qualities they want at minimum cost.

Core Values

But changing our vision is not without costs. It can cause insecurity, frustration, resentment, and, for those who lose their jobs, economic hardship. It is no wonder that new developments in the marketplace often produce reactionaries who try to block them. These reactionaries are the spiritual successors to the Luddites, the 18th-century British laborers who destroyed machines in a short-sighted and unsuccessful attempt to save their jobs. Fortunately for the world, the Luddites failed. If their vision had prevailed, most of us would still be laboring from dawn to dusk in dangerous, back-breaking jobs, with little to show for it.

Change destroys jobs. But it also creates new ones. Candlemakers have been replaced by electricians and natural gas manufacturers. Blacksmiths have given way to automobile and airplane mechanics. And here is a more recent instance of how change can bring unexpected benefits: Employees at one Koch Industries plant thought of so many new and better ways to improve performance that we were able to cut our maintenance force by 20 percent, or about 50 employees. But we didn't lay them off. Instead, we offered them the chance to create their own new jobs. The employees in question got together and decided to form an internal construction service group that would compete against all outside contractors. The group has been a terrific success, providing better, faster, and cheaper service. Imagine if AT&T and other American businesses that have recently resorted to massive layoffs tried this innovative, market-based approach. Who knows what new companies, products, and services they might create!

It is also possible to minimize resistance to change and greatly reduce hardship by establishing a culture based on certain core values, which are the second key dimension of Market-Based Management®. Values, like vision, help determine behavior.

Humility

We must acknowledge our weaknesses, identify what we don't know, and learn from others. Humility is essential to social progress since learning begins with the recognition that none of us has all the answers. Arrogance, the opposite of humility, has been one of man's greatest stumbling blocks. As historian Daniel Boorstin notes, "The greatest obstacle to discovery is not ignorance, it is the illusion of knowledge." Columbus's voyages were delayed for years because those in power "knew" the earth was flat. More recently, many people "knew" that airplanes would never fly.

In business, arrogance is equally destructive. In the 1960s and 1970s, American car manufacturers "knew" what American car buyers wanted and how to make the best cars. But the Japanese had different ideas. Likewise, many oil companies in the 1970s "knew" that the price of oil was going to $100 per barrel and made huge investments relying on that certainty. As the old saying goes, it isn't so much what we don't know that hurts us as it is what we know that isn't so.

Integrity

Dealing honestly and honoring commitments are also prerequisites of social progress and economic prosperity. The trust that integrity creates lowers the transaction costs of human interaction and is necessary to the exchange of knowledge. We must face reality rather than delude ourselves. There are several factors that make this more difficult than it sounds. The first, as I have pointed out, is the role of vision in learning. Until we open up our vision of what is possible and how the world works it is impossible for us to see reality and learn from it. Albert Einstein wrote: "Whether you can observe a thing depends on the theory [vision] you use"—not the other way around. Another factor is self interest. We all tend to rationalize away unpleasant or threatening ideas and facts.

Intellectual honesty and truth are at a minimum in command systems. The rulers develop a vision that the truth is whatever they say it is: The ruled initially are afraid to speak their minds but soon accept the vision of infallibility of the rulers. The creation of knowledge grinds to a halt, and progress ceases. This is as true for command-based business organizations as for political regimes.

Truth should be what stands the test of evidence and criticism, not what authorities say is true. A discovery culture based on honesty, openness, and constructive challenge improves and expands our knowledge, thinking, and vision.

Tolerance

Tolerance means treating others with dignity and respect. We cannot have a civil society unless we are willing to cooperate and learn from those with different kinds of knowledge and different perspectives. For example, it is easy to dismiss folk medicine as silly superstition. But medical researchers have discovered some truth in what we tend to dismiss as "old wives' tales." People in Peru used to chew the bark of the cinchona tree to reduce the effects of malaria. Today, we know that this bark contains quinine, which, until fairly recently, was the standard medical treatment for malaria.

In business, tolerance allows us to learn from others and improve—to share and integrate knowledge. To be successful, a company cannot forego ideas and talent just because they are different.

Responsibility

Taking responsibility for our own actions—rather than blaming others or being victims—is also vital to social progress. Only if we have the self-discipline to accept responsibility for our mistakes will we learn from them.

When, in response to deteriorating business, a company blames outside forces or covers up its problems by changing its accounting methods or by using other tricks, it ensures failure. When an employee covers up or blames others for problems, both trust and knowledge are lost, and the employee fails to develop and improve.

Desire to Contribute

Making a real contribution requires passion, initiative, and dedication. It also requires the discipline to profit only by economic rather than political means—that is, by the creation rather than the transfer of wealth. Economic profits are a measure of the value created in society, a sort of receipt for public service. In contrast, political profits—profits from government subsidies, restrictions on competition, or barriers to entry—are an indication of the destruction of value and of public disservice.

The same principles apply to employees as to firms. Employees must believe they have potential, that they can and want to contribute, and that they should be rewarded accordingly. They must look at their jobs not as routine tasks to endure but as opportunities to contribute, develop, and grow.

Long-Term Perspective

Being willing to make sacrifices or investments to build a better future is also important. In the history of this country, immigrant families have risen from poverty to the extent they sacrificed by working and saving to educate their children. Learning and self-development likewise involve sacrifice and require putting a higher value on the future than on the present.

The same is true for business. To last, a company must strive to add long-term value rather than going for the quick buck. This means that its behavior must be guided by the desire for continued relations with its principal constituencies—employees, customers, suppliers, stockholders, and communities. For example, at Koch Industries we have made it a practice to reinvest 90 percent of our profits into our companies.

Core values build trust, stimulate experimentation, and encourage the development of knowledge. They make people want to contribute. They are reinforced by hiring, training, men-

toring, promoting, and compensating. Most of all, they reinforced by strong examples; the leaders of the companies with
core values tend to practice what they preach. It is hardly
surprising, therefore, that a recent study found that the companies with core values grew sevenfold over an eight-year period, while those without had zero growth.

Incentives and Decision Rights

The third dimension of Market-Based Management® is an
incentive system that rewards accomplishment—a system that,
just as for entrepreneurs in society, enables employees to partici-
pate in the value they create. To be effective, incentives must
be based on more than employees' contributions to current
profits. Incentives must also consider contributions to long-
term success, including contributions to our culture and our
communities.

As employees contribute to long-term success, they acquire
"decision rights." Decision rights, the fourth dimension of
Market-Based Management®, refer to the level of responsibility and authority employees have to allocate their firms'
resources. In the marketplace, when entrepreneurs contribute they earn profits that give them additional property rights—
that is, the ability to direct more scarce resources. Market-Based
Management® attempts to duplicate this powerful market
process of moving control of resources to those who successfully satisfy customer needs.

This framework provides insights that are particularly significant in a world characterized by rapid change. For instance, it has become quite common in management literature
to critique top-down decisionmaking as inefficient. And, indeed,
centrally driven command and control corporations do experience the same type of problems as centrally planned economies. However, universal decentralization has its own set of
problems. There is no question that a firm wants to capture
the ideas and creativity of all its employees. But decisions
should be made by those with the *best* knowledge, which will

vary with the type of decision. For example, in the oil business, decisions on how to operate a pipeline to get the most "throughput" should be made locally, but decisions about how to integrate that pipeline with supply, sales, and trading need to be made by those with broader knowledge.

Knowledge Systems

The fifth and final dimension of Market-Based Management®—knowledge systems—is based on a woefully underappreciated mechanism for creating knowledge: market transactions. In a free economy, a primary function of prices and of profits and losses is to reveal what consumers value and the availability and utility of resources.

In the same manner, for a company to create a discovery process for employees to know what to do without being told, they must likewise have profit signals, or "discovery measures," so that employees can see what creates value and what does not. Just as for entrepreneurs in society, the proper measures expand employees' vision, change their thinking, and enable them to make new discoveries. These measures must include contributions to the whole, not just to one part. For example, measures that track the cost of failures in reliability, including lost profit from "down time," loss of credibility with customers, and environmental and safety problems, provide employees with a vision that is vastly superior to the typical one of controlling maintenance costs.

But, as important as knowledge systems are in bringing to bear the best knowledge, they won't work unless decision-makers possess core values. Modern technology transmits information with incredible speed, but that doesn't do much good in a culture that stifles learning. Anticipating or even keeping up with rapid change requires the effective integration of knowledge, and that can only be done in an open, sharing, and adapting culture.

From our efforts to apply this integrated framework at Koch, we have a new vision of employees. In this vision, employees don't have jobs; rather, they have a set of rights, responsibilities, and rewards that enable them to best contribute.

Helping People

What Market-Based Management® is all about is helping people fulfill their potential.

It is about helping everyone develop the vision, values, and desire to better their lives by making a contribution.

It is about enabling people to do good by doing well.

As you might suspect, understanding and implementing Market-Based Management® is not easy, and we at Koch Industries are far from where we want to be. In fact, I would say that we are about a "4" on a scale of 1 to 10. But even that modest progress has enabled us to grow *over one-hundredfold in the last 30 years,* and to be growing and hiring today while many of our competitors are shrinking and laying people off.

And Market-Based Management® is not just for large companies or even for adults. As we have learned in our work with at-risk high school students, everyone has the potential to develop and contribute. One of the students in our Young Entrepreneurs program, April Sheldon, says:

> When I was younger, I had some people tell me there were certain things I couldn't do because I already had three strikes against me. I was black, I was female, and I didn't have any money. I don't believe that anymore.... Now I know that I can become financially independent if I apply the entrepreneurial concepts I have learned and if I work hard.

April's path is open to everyone, given the right environment. We have the opportunity to help create that environment, to help clear that path. I have taken this as a personal challenge and welcome those who would like to join me. By focusing on the right framework, vision, and values, we can make the world a better place for everyone.

ANDREA MILLEN RICH

How to Succeed in Business Using Market Methods

I am not an intellectual or a pundit. I have no new business principles which will amaze you. My full topic is "How to Succeed in Business Using Market Methods," but frankly, I don't know any other way.

Mine is a small, ideological business with a particular niche: people interested in free market economics and individualist political theory. It is called Laissez Faire Books, and it is a division of a nonprofit educational foundation, Center for Independent Thought. But it is run strictly as a business; we don't have donors: the people we have to satisfy are our customers. In the previous year, Laissez Faire Books' volume was $1.5 million, so that makes it a fairly representative "small business."

Define Your Mission

Critical to the success of any business is defining its mission. Incorporated in our mission is the only evidence of our nonprofit status: to put books on liberty into the hands of as many people as possible without losing money. We announce on our front page: "World's largest selection of books on liberty."

But we are not in business just to sell books; we want to develop customers. Selling books is a one-time thing; the goal is to maximize the number of books sold. *Our* goal, however, is to maximize the number of readers who are interested in the books we sell. It costs too much money to mail to people who aren't interested in our books. We need people on whom we can depend and who can depend on us.

At Laissez Faire Books, we are in an unusual position. Our customers have a stake in our success. They are really rooting for us. And if we succeed, it says something about all of us. It means the ideas of liberty are being accepted and are important to people.

Keep Your Word

I never took an economics course. My parents had a small business and what I learned from them was to keep your word to both your customers and your suppliers: Do what you say you're going to do, and pay your bills. Everything else I know about business I learned from my husband, Howie, who worked with me closely when we first bought Laissez Faire Books in 1982. Here, I'd like to share some details of the early years of the company since I believe that they are common to the experience of so many small businesses.

John Muller and Sharon Presley created Laissez Faire Books in 1972 as a bookstore with a mail-order feature. As Sharon wrote in the 20th anniversary issue of the catalogue:

> I did see our job to be, as Albert Jay Nock put it, taking care of the Remnant, the Remnant who care about freedom, individual rights, individualism, the Remnant who want to build a new society with "liberty and justice for all." To build a new society requires changing ideas. Not laws, not voting, not just political activism, but changing ways of thinking. And to change ideas, you need ideas, and arguments, and information, and most of all, a moral and philosophical framework.

The Remnant responded to some extent, and Laissez Faire Books grew and became important to all sorts of people. The company did not aim mainly at academics but at the independent intellectual interested in liberty and individualism in many different aspects. Therefore, the bookstore and the catalogue offered fiction, humor, and other works, not just economics texts by the likes of Austrian School founders Ludwig von Mises and Carl Menger.

The mail-order catalog grew. After a few years Sharon left to get her doctorate in psychology. Current Hillsdale College Professor Richard Ebeling, who was studying at New York University at the time, picked up the slack with the catalogue and did most of the reviews. The emphasis shifted, given Richard's interests, to politics and economics. Remember, there was very little new libertarian political and economic writing available at the time, but Laissez Faire Books featured all of it.

The company was always undercapitalized, and even though John had his best year in 1980 with a volume of sales reaching $100,000, the drain of maintaining inventory and producing and distributing the catalog became too much. At some point in 1981, having exhausted all his possible loan partners, John decided he would have to close shop.

Learn from Your Mistakes

My husband and I bought the assets (a tiny inventory by then, some unfilled orders, and a mailing list of 4,500 names). We immediately created a very elegant—and very costly— mailing, informing all of our customers of the change in ownership and announcing several exciting new books like Thomas Sowell's *Ethnic America* and Murray Rothbard's *Ethics of Liberty*. The envelope of our expensive mailing was mistakenly printed touting Rothbard's *Ethnics of Liberty*. Fortunately, we discovered the error in time and reprinted the envelopes, but it was an expense we could hardly afford.

Indeed, sometimes little mistakes can cost a business a lot. Some of our subsequent typos haven't been caught so quickly. A few years ago, one of my managing editors prided herself on catching every typo. In her nearly three years of service, she made only one error, but it was a doozy: Instead of offering 10 percent discount to customers who deposited $225 with us, one month we offered the 10 percent off to anyone who sent us $25!

Control Your Costs

Howie and I poured a lot of money into Laissez Faire Books in the first few years. Sales grew, the customer base grew, our margin grew. Howie taught me to be a tough negotiator. We pay on average 50 percent less for books than John and Sharon paid. That's one important way we are able to stay in business and generate surpluses rather than deficits by the end of the year.

It is impossible to overstress the importance of controlling costs. Hold firm to this principle. If you don't, you won't stay in business. At Laissez Faire Books, if we say, "This book is important, and we'll pay 50 cents more than we can afford and make it up elsewhere," our margin will inevitably slip, and there will be no way to restore it.

If we pay more than we should for rent or utilities or a costlier computer system than is warranted for our particular business, we'll also get into deep trouble. This doesn't mean that we should be cheap. It means we should be prudent and weigh costs and benefits objectively. This is why we are now strictly a mail-order business, and our money goes into our monthly bulletin, customer service personnel, and toll-free telephone service instead of into a fancy store or offices.

Take Risks

Another requirement of success is taking risks. You can't succeed by being risk averse—after all, just starting a business is a tremendous gamble. As an entrepreneur, you must be willing to stand by your decisions even when there is no guarantee that they are right. For example, many publishers have offered to sell us books on consignment so that we only pay for what we sell and return the leftovers. That would certainly lower our risk, but we would also receive a smaller discount. So we willingly assume the risk, and we never buy books on consignment.

Test Your Product

Business leaders, especially in the field of marketing, say that testing is very important—and it is. You should examine what other businesses are doing and learn from them. For instance, in the mail-order book business, most catalogues are printed on newsprint. It looks lousy, but it works. I tested better paper, but the results were actually poorer. That's right: The good paper cost more, but it generated less in sales. I didn't believe this at first. I assumed the mailer must have gotten the test lists mixed up, so I retested and seeded both sections of the list to make sure there was no mix-up. But the second test produced the same result. We got better absolute numbers with the cheaper paper. It must be because this is the industry standard. People who plead with me to print a finer quality bulletin will have to prove to me that it will pay off.

Trust Your Instincts

But sometimes you have to bet on yourself. Someone once observed that the direct mail industry is counter-intuitive, and I think that's partly true. That is why occasional testing of ideas, products, and service is advisable. However when the situation involves a major business decision, I often tend to "go with my gut." I am not being willful or impetuous; I am relying on my experience and trusting my instincts.

Customer Service

Customer service is taking a larger portion of our attention, and I think that is true for businesses everywhere. You must have a fine product of which you are proud, and then you must take care of your customers. There is a lot of competition in business today. You will make mistakes just as everyone does. It is how you handle the mistakes that counts. It is making sure that the person who speaks to your unhappy customer wants to *solve* the problem and wants to turn the encounter into an opportunity to develop closer ties. For us at Laissez Faire Books, it also means having knowledgeable employees who can help a customer find the most comprehensive book on free market environmentalism or call to mind the name of the author who wrote on tariffs in 1892.

Be Part of the Revolution

We mail over a million pieces a year to more than 90 countries around the world. We like to think that we are part of the revolution that has swept the world, challenged socialism and the omnipotent state, and rediscovered individual rights and the free market. Last summer I met a young man from Bucharest, Romania, who was in the United States attending an economic seminar. He seemed quite well-read in the field of free market economics, and he volunteered that his hero was Ludwig von Mises. I asked where he had studied. He explained that about a year and a half earlier he had wandered into the Laissez Faire Books corner in a Bucharest bookstore and picked up Mises' *Human Action*. It transformed his life: He was going to be an engineer, but now he wants to be an economist and save his country.

Later that summer, Rakesh Wadhwa from Katmandu, Nepal, came by to show me the book he had written about freeing up the economy of India. He had begun with some of the books in our catalogue: Ayn Rand's *Capitalism, The Unknown Ideal* and Milton Friedman's *Free To Choose* and *Capi-*

talism and Freedom. Rakesh is challenging years of socialist ideology in India, and we were able to provide some of the ammunition.

Define What Success Means to You

So, if I am so smart, why isn't Laissez Faire Books an even bigger success? I haven't figured that out yet. Our original goal was 100,000 customers within 10 years, but, 14 years later, we have only about 30,000. Sometimes I don't see how we will ever get to 100,000, but we won't give up on expanding. Though Barnes & Noble and Walden Books aren't trembling at the prospect of competing with us, and though we have found out that there really is a limited ideological market for books, we have also discovered that we can prosper and grow and fulfill our mission.

In the last ten years, our most phenomenal best-seller was Barbara Branden's *The Passion of Ayn Rand.* We sold 6,000 copies the year it appeared. Although Rand's books are available everywhere, we have sold a total of 6,100 copies of *Atlas Shrugged.* Last year alone, we sold over 2,000 copies of F. A. Hayek's *The Road to Serfdom.* We can sell at least 3,000 of any of Thomas Sowell's books. We have sold 8,000 copies of Rose Wilder Lane's *Discovery of Freedom* and about the same number of Frederic Bastiat's *The Law.*

But before you run out to buy a book business, let me hasten to assure you that not all our sales are so stellar. We sold 88 copies of *The Philosophy of the Austrian School* last year and only 32 copies of Frank Fetter's classic *Capital, Interest, and Rent.* And speaking of classics, we sold only 21 copies of Jane Jacobs's *Death and Life of Great American Cities.* Since 1986, we have sold 2,500 copies of *Anarchy, State, and Utopia* by Robert Nozick, but only 410 *Basic Works of Aristotle.* Sometimes we don't know why one book sells and another doesn't. We only sold 56 copies of John Locke's *Two Treatises of Government* last year, but 673 copies of the *Federalist.*

We have positioned ourselves for another possible growth spurt. Our biggest coup, and my most important achievement at Laissez Faire Books, has been negotiating paperback rights to Ludwig von Mises's *Human Action* so that we can make it available at an affordable price. It is now being used in several college classrooms around the country. We have sold 7,000 paperback copies since 1991 and our rights have been extended through the year 2000.

Now, we have just obtained rights to the 50th anniversary edition of Henry Hazlitt's great *Economics in One Lesson.* We sell between 3,000 and 3,500 copies of this book every year, year after year. It has introduced more people to the principles of the free market than any other book I know. Hazlitt, of course, was an eminent economic journalist and I wanted a new introduction by someone in an analogous position. Recently, Steve Forbes faxed me a brilliant, moving introduction that references Mises, Hayek, and Bastiat. The Forbes introduction to this simple but profound little book with the wonderful title will justify advertising it like crazy. Now *here's* a place to invest money! And obviously we expect a fair amount of free publicity for the anniversary edition, too. All this means new names—my goal is 10,000 new names—which we hope to convert into new customers. So Laissez Faire is coming full circle.

Love What You Do

The final advice I have for you is: Love what you do. You spend so much time at your work: Find something that is stimulating and rewarding and give it everything you've got. That's what I do, and I couldn't be happier.

GEORGE ROCHE

Capitalism and the Future of America

The brilliant economist George Gilder has written that the most important event in recent history is "the demise of socialist dream." However, he also notes "the failure of capitalism to win a corresponding triumph." Why is this so, when capitalism has so obviously provided more material benefits for every individual, regardless of economic or social condition, than any other system in the history of the world? Why, when capitalism's intellectual defense has been so ably undertaken by some of the greatest minds of our time is socialism, thinly disguised, still taught in our schools and promoted by our politicians? And why, when capitalism's results are so demonstrably humanitarian, is it still seen as a symbol for greed and exploitation?

Ideas Have Consequences

The perplexing answers to these questions share a common root: They all lie in the realm of ideas. Ideas, I find myself often saying, rule the world—not armies, not economics, not politics, not any of the things to which we usually give our allegiance, but ideas. "Ideas have consequences"—in just three words University of Chicago Professor Richard Weaver encapsulated an entire philosophy of life that is also a challenge, a call to action for all of us. Throughout history there have been formative "moments in time" in which particular ideas and particular leaders exert a profound impact on the character and events of a nation. These special epochs, marked by the emergence of a new consensus, can readily be found in American history. It is important to look at the past because I believe that there we will find the answers to so many modern day problems, including the problems of American business.

America's First "Moment in Time"

The first great "moment in time" that created a virtual sea-change in American society occurred 150 years before the American Revolution, in an era when our colonial ancestors enjoyed a large measure of self-government. From the start, the American colonial experience had drawn heavily upon the traditional liberties of British subjects and upon their rich heritage of individual freedom guaranteed by the Magna Carta.

By the eighteenth century, however, the British were pursuing a different goal. A new economic idea, "mercantilism," dominated British thinking. Government planning and control regulated society and manipulated individuals. Eventually, the American colonists ran out of patience with this growing governmental interference in their affairs. During the summer of 1776, Thomas Jefferson wrote the Declaration of Independence, a revolutionary document destined to represent liberty for the American republic as long as it should endure.

Coincidentally, during that same summer in 1776, a book was published thousands of miles away from the colonies, a book destined to have a profound effect on America. The author, Adam Smith, was a professor of moral philosophy at the University of Glasgow, and the book was *The Wealth of Nations*. As a moral philosopher, Smith contended that men must be free to make their own decisions because, if they are not, a moral paralysis soon sets in. From this basic truth, he examined mercantilism and discovered that this early form of the planned economy was denying men freedom of choice and thus distorting British society.

Eleven years later, fifty-five men met in Philadelphia to draft our Constitution. Motivated primarily by the ideas articulated by Jefferson and Smith, our Founding Fathers charted our national path toward limited government, the dignity of free men, and the marvelous prosperity we have enjoyed in this country.

America's Second "Moment in Time"

The next great "moment in time" and resulting sea-change in our nation's history occurred in the late 19th and early 20th century. Unfortunately, the new ideas that were promoted favored the collective over the individual, redirecting America on an increasingly hazardous path. The setting was ripe. For years, as America's industries boomed, immigrants poured in, and cities mushroomed, it began to seem to some that the scale of life itself had so magnified that the common man no longer had a fair chance to get ahead in the world.

Far from what one might expect, however, the momentum for collectivism was imparted not by public figures but by little-known men of ideas whose names not one in a hundred Americans would recognize. In certain elite circles, some wondered whether the answers for America's growing pains might not lie elsewhere than in the common sense of the Founding Fathers and the time-tested traditions of our Judeo-Christian heritage—and whether those answers might not instead be found in the work of certain "daring" European thinkers like Marx, Darwin, and Freud, whose ideas had rocked the Old World during the 1800s.

So a relative handful of professors and intellectuals, writing in the first years of this century and drawing on iconoclastic theories already well advanced in Europe, brought those ideas to America. And they thus began a process that remade the face of American society within thirty years, roughly between 1900 and 1930. These collectivist ideas spread from a few seminal thinkers, to the second- and third-hand purveyors of ideas—teachers, ministers, the working press, i.e., the word wielders. The collective mentality continued to spread, reaching the professions, the business community, the courts, the novelists, the artists, the general public, and last—always last—the politicians.

Of the first seminal thinkers of the new era, John Dewey has had a lasting impact on our philosophy, our education, our culture, and, ultimately, our government. From his "progressive school" experiment of the mid-1890s at the University of Chicago, Dewey advocated a system of education which would produce a new generation of Americans with a preference for group and social activity and who viewed themselves not as individuals but as members of a "total democratic society." He emphasized the unfinished nature of society and the universe and called for "a new kind of religion" to be derived from human experience and relationships.

Dewey's intellectual colleagues were themselves busy on other fronts. At Columbia, anthropologist Ruth Benedict and her mentor Franz Boas were developing the ideas that man could be understood only as a social animal, since his character was allegedly the exclusive creation of his society and environment. Charles Beard's *An Economic Interpretation of the Constitution* was another key turning point. He set aside the traditional ideas of American society in favor of an essentially Marxian philosophy of history in which the Founding Fathers were portrayed as having placed the economic welfare of a few ahead of the total social welfare of all.

The flamboyant Thorstein Veblen poured out his bitter frustration on the business community in shrill diatribes like *The Theory of the Leisure Class.* Meanwhile, Veblen's fellow economists John R. Commons and Richard Ely pioneered in charting a vastly expanded role for organized labor in the new collectivity. Sociologist Lester Frank Ward, one of the true patron saints of the modern American collectivist ideal, saw politics as a manipulating device designed to control all society, stating: "Modern society is suffering from the very opposite of paternalism—from under-government." In Ward, all those years ago, we thus find the original germ of an idea that has been central to the social planner's rhetoric from the New Deal era to the Clinton era.

By 1932, the year the arch-collectivist and political pragmatist Franklin D. Roosevelt was elected president, the intellectual revolutionaries had already done their work, and they rapidly became the new political establishment. Under FDR, the new generation of intellectuals managed to use the Depression as a pretext for a massive collectivization of American society throughout the decade of the 1930s. They failed to cure the Depression, but a "fortunate" circumstance—World War II—did it for them. After the war, the social engineers stood ready with further collectivist gimmicks such as the Full Employment Act of 1946.

Ratifying Collectivist Inroads

There was steady pressure throughout the Truman years for major expansion of the federal role in health, in education, and in welfare—pressure that finally resulted in new government programs under the succeeding Republican president, Dwight D. Eisenhower. Eisenhower proved once again that Republican administrations usually ratify rather than reverse the collectivist inroads of their Democratic predecessors. The same pattern of ratification and acceleration was repeated two decades later when the Nixon and Ford administrations helped consolidate most of Lyndon Johnson's Great Society programs, exacerbated the oil crisis and other economic woes through an unprecedented program of peacetime wage-and-price controls, and presided over the regulatory explosion of the early 1970s.

In the last months of the Reagan presidency, we wondered if the pattern had been repeated. Many saw Reagan's election in 1980 and his subsequent reelection in 1984 as genuine evidence of Americans' disenchantment with government—a disenchantment that cut across ideological lines and was an inevitable reaction to the love affair with statism that has been carried on for so long. But whatever one thinks in retrospect of Reagan's actual accomplishments, it is uncertain whether much has changed. Critics on the left have declared that the end of the Reagan era signaled the end of conservatism's brief resurgence. Even after the stunning Republican victories in the 1994 elections, they still regard conservatism as an anomaly that will inevitably be "corrected."

The Fundamental Principle of Freedom

Undeniably the idea of capitalism, a central tenet of conservatism, remains under constant assault, and its detractors comprise a majority in our schools, our media, and even our political and cultural leadership communities. One faction we may dub the "anti-capitalists," those who regard the redistribution of wealth in the name of "economic justice" as the proper goal of all economic activity. Many anti-capitalists claim that modern capitalism began with the Industrial Revolution and heralded child labor, wage slavery, urban squalor, and a Hobbesian existence for the working class. The late 20th century, they insist, is still an era of exploitation.

A second group focuses less on capitalism's evils than its supposed inadequacies. It is all right to defend free enterprise, so the reasoning goes, but today there are simply too many demands on the system—too many poor, too many problems, too many inequities—for individuals or the free market to handle. Government must, therefore, step in and act as the problem-solver. Far more people belong to this group than the first. They have accepted the need for intervention even though they may harbor no outright hostility to capitalism.

Both groups are obsessively results-oriented. They begin with the premise that the world is perfectible and that man possesses the means to perfect it through his own reason and through man-made institutions. Capitalism simply cannot fulfill their expectations. Yet no amount of intellect and no economic system—no man-made system at all, for that matter—can cure every ill the world produces; it probably can't even cure half of them. Sadly, the false notion persists that some other system, some other grand vision, can achieve the impossible.

What we must remember is that the central idea of capitalism does not lie in the miracle of the market or even the ingenuity of the entrepreneur. It rests, rather, on the fundamental principle of freedom. One of the great sources of strength for America has been our commitment to economic, political, and religious freedom. Within our open society, individuals are free to provide for themselves and their families, to compete with others and to join with them in voluntary associations. We have been free to support those professions, businesses, schools, hospitals, churches, and cultural institutions which best meet our individual needs and preferences. In other words, we have prospered with competition and voluntary association in the private sector.

The American economy, despite its ups and downs and the serious threats it faces from overregulation, the deficit, and the other problems of our times, has worked beautifully—beyond the wildest dreams of the utopian social planners. But it has worked precisely because we have allowed individuals to act freely on their own.

Self-Transcendence

Self-transcendence is the ability to rise above the merely animal, merely physical self, and freely choose the conditions and terms of our own existence; to decide what is of ultimate importance and act upon it whether or not other people understand, whether or not it is dangerous, whether or not it makes us rich. Only human beings have that capacity. Only you and I do. We have the capacity to rise above our merely physical selves. Self-transcendence, based on individual choice, touches every aspect of our lives.

If economic transactions were based on the immediate cave-man rip-off—the idea that I want to grab all I can get, and I want to get it right now, and I will not honor any obligation that interferes with this—no long-term economic planning would be possible. No investment, nothing of what we call a capital structure, could ever come into existence, unless legal contracts were honored. So we need self-transcending people, people willing to honor their commitments.

All civilization is based upon the integrity of the self-responsible individual, directed by a view of justice, of restraint, and of responsibility. There was a time when this country of ours valued such an idea. It placed its faith in the responsible individual and the institutional structure, giving form to our lives. And it is the erosion of that faith which today destroys us from within. I submit to you that unless we recover it, all the methods in the world to do something better economically, technologically, or socially are just so much spitting in the wind.

America's Third Moment in Time

The good news is that the long-awaited opportunity to create another "moment in time" is finally here. The right ideas and the right leaders are beginning to come together. The failure of public welfare, public education, and other examples of statism has led to a tremendous resurgence of traditional values—values that give primacy to the freedom and dignity of the individual. And the fall of the Berlin Wall and the nearly worldwide collapse of communism has provided undeniable proof that capitalism is the only system that leaves people free. But even more important, more and more people are beginning to realize that capitalism is good not because it works, but rather that it works because it is good—because it has the fundamentally proper view of human nature.

But opportunities do not last forever, and the time to seize them passes swiftly. As the great Christian apologist C. S. Lewis put it, "You can't go on being a good egg forever. Sooner or later you have to hatch or rot." Well, most of us are well on the way to one or the other of those fates. But we still have the God-given power to choose which it will be. We can just sit and rot, or we can hatch. We can build a society that hatches, too—at this, America's third "moment in time."

HARRY E. TEASLEY, JR.

Thriving in the Future

There are three broad themes that I think will be important to thriving in the future and ensuring the prosperity of
our nation. The first theme deals with *complexity, change, and
collapsing time horizons.* We are living in a complex, interdependent world characterized by global products and global
financial markets. And one only needs to look at the electronics and computer industries to appreciate the collapsing
nature of time horizons where innovative new products are
often obsolete within a few years. In this kind of world, corporations and individuals must be fast, flexible, and focused.

A second major theme that characterizes the future is *competition.* In today's global economy, no markets are immune to
intense competition. Protectionists may argue that we should
erect walls around our economy, but no matter how high we
build them they will come crashing down of their own accord. In the competitive environment of the 1990s, we must
concentrate instead on being creative and innovative. Uphold-
ing the "status quo" simply won't do.

Keeping free enterprise free is the third theme, and it is also a
prerequisite if we are to thrive in the future. We must strengthen
our commitment to individual freedom, private property, and
free markets rather than statist, regulatory government. To
understand why this is so important, think of a track meet
in which there are two 400-meter races. The first is the mid-

distance sprint, which has been run in a record time of 43.29 seconds. Equate this race to the normal pace of business. The second is the intermediate hurdle race in which the competitors must clear 10 hurdles that are 35 meters apart. Equate these to government regulations. The intermediate hurdle race has been run in a record time of 46.72 seconds, or about 3.4 seconds slower than the sprint. Obviously, there is a cost—in terms of time, resources, and energy—for competitors who must jump over obstacles placed in their path. In the race that is business, government regulations are the obstacles.

There is also another comparison that can be made between governmental regulations and the hurdles of a track race. No single runner has ever dominated the mid-distance sprint, yet the great athlete Edwin Moses went undefeated for over nine years in the 400-meter hurdle race. To be a world-class hurdler, one must be able to take exactly 13 steps between hurdles, and only Edwin Moses was able to do so consistently. If the hurdles had been closer or farther apart, things might have been different. Government regulations always offer some individuals and businesses an advantage and others a disadvantage. While they are often proposed or enacted with the objective of generating a benefit (which may or may not be achieved), it is important to recognize that they make markets less free and more political.

Two Competing Worldviews

You and I stand at a watershed in world history. We have been witness to the failure of a 70-plus-year experiment in socialism, central planning, and governmental intervention that failed in its attempt to produce wealth and prosperity just as it failed to produce individual freedom and such benefits as civil rights and environmental protection. Yet government regulation in the U.S. is currently expanding at an exponential rate. Why? Because, even after the failure of central planning in Eastern Europe and Soviet Union, there are still two powerful but opposing belief systems at play in the Western world.

Their differences are most dramatically revealed in one area of global concern: the environment. The first belief system belongs to the "green movement." Its advocates—mostly large environmental organizations and leftist environmentalists— charge that environmental problems result from market failure. They regard economic freedom as incompatible with environmental values, goals, and objectives, and they rely upon political solutions through collective action, central planning, and command-and-control regulatory approaches. In addition, they believe that only they should decide what products are produced and that all information relevant to their cause should be centralized through huge data-gathering operations.

The second belief system is the basis of "free market environmentalism." Its advocates—mostly businesses and political conservatives—believe that the failure to create markets, due to government intervention, is a chief cause of not only environmental problems but many other problems in our society. They argue, for instance, that the recent S&L fiasco was largely due to government intervention and Federal Deposit Insurance. Market corrections would have been much faster and the outcome would have been far less costly if savings and loan institutions had been to forced to compete in a free market economy and had been required to purchase insurance privately while being rated by private rating agencies.

"The Tragedy of the Commons"

When it comes to what system best protects the environment, many free marketers cite the concept of the "commons." In a 1968 issue of *Science* magazine, University of California biologist Garrett Hardin published an essay titled, "The Tragedy of the Commons." Drawing upon the observations of the ancient Greek philosopher Aristotle, Hardin described a tribal society that earned its living by grazing sheep on common grasslands. For years, the population of sheep never increased to the point of overgrazing. But then the tribe developed institutions like cities and health services to extend life. With those institutions and that stability came more people and more sheep.

As the number of sheep increased, the grazing began to approach the natural carrying capacity of the grasslands, and the grasslands began to degrade. Each individual looked at the situation and elected to increase his own wealth by putting one more sheep onto the commons. The positive value of the extra sheep accrued to the individual while the negative value of the sheep was distributed proportionally to all his neighbors, as well as himself. His neighbors were rational and they, too, elected to put more sheep on the commons— only to increase the damage to the grasslands.

This was the "tragedy of the commons." No single individual was responsible for the common resource, yet everyone exploited it. No one was willing to conserve unilaterally or to invest in the commons since the benefits of the investment would be distributed among everyone. One of possible resolutions Hardin discussed was mutual coercion, or democratic socialism. For the last 25 years, we have used this model to discuss and understand environmental issues. This prescription has also been used to promote complex administrative law and regulations to deal with the environment.

There was, however, another alternative for addressing the tragedy of the commons. The grasslands could have been divided and privatized so that individuals had ownership and stewardship—responsibility for a piece of what had been held in common. In this situation, the benefits and the risks of investment in an individual's property would accrue to that individual and not to free riders.

The Example of Consumer Packaging

Through the "lens" of one specific environmental issue, consumer packaging, it may be demonstrated how these two world-

views—the green movement and free market environmentalism—actually work.

For decades now, green organizations and activists have push-
ed to regulate and limit the use of packaging materials. They
claim:

- plastic packaging should be banned because it is made
  from a nonrenewable resource;

- multi-layered packaging should be banned because some
  view it to be nonrecyclable;

- all packages should be made of materials having a specified
  minimum recyclable content;

- government should specify materials and packages for
  specific end-use.

They have succeed in convincing politicians that these and
many of their other claims are valid. At all levels of government, literally thousands of legislative and regulatory proposals
have been introduced to manage packaging, raw materials,
solid waste, and recycling. These are often contradictory, discriminatory, and unlikely to meet their professed objectives.

The "rush to regulate" must be understood in the context
of Austrian School economist Friedrich A. Hayek's article, "The
Use of Knowledge in Society." In this landmark essay, which
appeared in a 1945 issue of the *American Economic Journal,* Hayek
argues that data and the knowledge of circumstances never
exist in a concentrated or integrated form but solely as dispersed bits of incomplete and frequently contradictory knowledge possessed by separate individuals. In other words, each
of us possesses limited knowledge. We have to combine it with
the knowledge of others in order to achieve progress. Following from this, Hayek argues that the main economic problem
in society is the utilization of knowledge, which can never
be given to anyone in its totality.

Let me discuss a personal odyssey in trying to develop data
and knowledge about a very small piece of the economy; namely,

soft-drink packaging. In 1970, my employer, the Coca-Cola Company, commissioned a research project to prepare an environmental impact analysis of eight different packages and packaging systems. Today, these studies are referred to as "life-cycle studies."

A little history might be useful as to why we undertook this study. In 1966–1967, we undertook a major review of our can procurement practices. Should we make cans or should we buy them? Several technologies were available. The three-piece soldered side-seam can represented a common technology easily available to any would-be producer. Continental Can had recently invented "Conoweld," a system for welding side seams; and American Can had invented and developed an adhesive-bonded side seam. Coors and Reynolds had either made investments or were considering investments in the manufacture of the two-piece drawn and ironed aluminum can.

It didn't take much analysis to conclude that the old, heavy three-piece can with the soldered side seam, manufactured from steel, tin, aluminum, and lead, was a nonstarter. The technology was already obsolete. Aluminum can technologies were in their infancy, and the welded and adhesive-bonded technologies were proprietary. So, in the end, we decided not to manufacture our cans. But that study was important for another reason, because it forced us to look at a number of other issues such as material availability and long-term opportunities for technological improvement through weight reduction and energy savings.

During this period I began to think that we needed a more sophisticated assessment process for evaluating our packaging. We were also deeply involved in a project to develop a plastic bottle for carbonated beverages. Early on in the process to develop this container, we were very aware of the fact that plastic bottles were manufactured from nonrenewable resources, i.e., hydrocarbons. Feedstocks were either oil or natural gas. Also about this time, public interest in environmental issues began to increase.

Building on the information which we had developed in the "can-make-or-buy" project, I concluded it was necessary for the Coca-Cola Company to do a total environmental impact analysis of plastic bottles before we went forward commercially—and to compare those impacts with alternative containers. So, in 1970, we commissioned the first environmental impact analysis for a set of consumer products. The results of that first study were both interesting and counterintuitive. Of particular interest was the energy analysis of plastic bottles as compared to glass bottles. Most of us think of glass as being made of a rather common material: sand. A systems analysis makes it obvious that energy is the major factor in the production of glass bottles, in both the manufacturing and the distribution processes.

One of the conclusions we reached was that there were actually fewer hydrocarbon resources used in the manufacture of the plastic bottle substitute we were developing than in the glass soft drink bottles we were using. This included the hydrocarbons extant in the bottle itself, which were still available for either conversion to energy or recycling as hydrocarbons. That piece of knowledge gave our company the confidence to proceed with the development and commercialization of the plastic now widely used in the soft drink beverage industry. And today we are producing it in a way that is far more efficient in terms of material and energy than when we began.

While our first environmental impact analysis was extremely useful, it was a very difficult study to perform. Nobody had ever attempted anything like it; it was a pioneering effort. Data gathering and understanding the interrelationships between processes and impacts were real challenges. It took over a year, at a substantial cost, to gather and analyze the results. But we did so because we needed the information to make specific decisions on allocating scarce resources.

Today, "green" environmentalists demand that all packages and all products be evaluated on a cradle-to-grave basis. The undertaking of such a task is simply mind-boggling and even if it could be accomplished, the data would be obsolete tomorrow. Overnight somebody will have invented something new that changes the status quo. Hayek was right: Information is dispersed, and the corollary is that decisionmaking should be dispersed to achieve efficiency in the economy. Cradle-to-grave studies may be useful for single companies, but they are simply inappropriate for industries—and they are a poor basis for making public policy decisions.

Several years ago the Northeast states from Maine to New York formed an organization called CONEG, or the Council of Northeast Governors. This council came together to discuss issues relating to solid waste, recycling, and packaging. At one point the council was on the verge of concluding that government should establish packaging specifications for all products. In fact, one of the first products that they considered was a product of great importance to the Coca-Cola Company —orange juice.

I was asked to present a paper on orange juice packaging. As I began my presentation, I was immediately challenged by a young woman who thought that I was essentially an immoral brigand for packaging orange juice. She said that the orange was the greatest example of a product that required no packaging and maintained that this was the way it should be sold.

But let us examine her thesis. At first glance, the fresh orange does appear to be an excellent example of a product that exemplifies the CONEG concept of *no packaging*. Upon closer examination, however, this is not the case. For example, commercial juice processors squeeze oranges far more efficiently than consumers because of the industrial equipment they use to perform the task. A consumer will, at a minimum, require about 20 percent more oranges than a processor to yield the same amount of juice. So, home squeezing of fresh oranges is a less efficient use of oranges and, therefore, a less efficient use of agricultural land, fertilizers, pesticides, water resources, agricultural capital, and agricultural labor than packaged orange juice.

And fresh oranges *do* require packaging. They are put in large, corrugated containers for distribution to retail outlets. In fact, fresh oranges generate almost nine times more corrugated waste than the frozen concentrate alternative. And, at the consumer level, fresh oranges generate over 60 times more waste (in terms of poundage). The waste is, of course, wet peels versus the small 12-ounce composite can containing frozen concentrate.

Then there is the issue of recycling. When a consumer squeezes oranges, the wet peels are disposed of through the solid waste collection and disposal system, while a juice processor converts the peel to animal feed and also recovers orange oil and d'limonene, which are used for other products and processes.

Fresh oranges also weigh about 7.5 times as much as the 12-ounce frozen concentrate alternative, and they require about 6.5 times as many trucks to distribute equal quantities of orange juice to the consumer. So, in addition to agricultural efficiencies, the frozen concentrate is more efficient when it comes to trucks, diesel fuel, and road systems.

The Example of Recycling

The eminent British classicist and essayist C. S. Lewis once wrote that we must be very careful to establish our priorities—to distinguish between "first and second things" lest we fail to achieve either. Is recycling a first or second thing? I argue that it is a second thing. It is merely a tactic or process we may use to achieve a more fundamental goal: efficient use of resources. But the green worldview focuses on recycling as an end in itself, and it does not recognize that recycling is not free. The process of recycling may require:

- the expenditure of energy;
- the use of process materials;
- labor inputs; and
- investments in capital facilities.

The competing worldview acknowledges that recycling must be judged on the basis of efficiency—efficiency of material, energy, labor, landfill space, and capital. But since it is impossible to be equally efficient in all these areas at once, how do we choose between them? How do we make trade-offs? In a market economy, there is a single mechanism through which we can make incommensurables commensurable: price.

Price has always dictated recycling decisions in the past. Rag merchants, scrap metal dealers, waste paper dealers, and junkyard operators have long participated in a wide variety of recycling activities for profit. Thousands of industrial and retail operations recycle effectively and efficiently because the economics are right. They are usually right because one of two conditions exists. Under the first condition, there is a large amount of uniform, sorted material being generated at one source. Under the second condition, as products are dispersed by the manufacturer, distributor, and retailer to consumer, they are desegregated and mixed. Recycling is then dependent upon collection, aggregation, appropriate sorting, and transportation.

If an economic analysis indicates that it doesn't make financial sense to recycle in a given circumstance, then that should be a red flag. It means that the recycling process is consuming too many costly resources. There are several other ways that this idea might be expressed: A recycling activity must yield a product that has economic value in commerce. Or, a recycling activity must use fewer resources and produce less waste than not recycling.

Today, there is a lot of talk about establishing "recycling goals" and objectives without an in-depth analysis of the trade-offs required to achieve them. There is much confusion about the definitions of "recycled products" and "recyclable material." The issues associated with defining recycled content are very complex. For example, it may be that a specific paper product can utilize a small amount of recycled material without dramatically affecting technical performance or cost; yet at a higher level of recycled content, the technical specifications may be dramatically degraded or the costs may be dramatically increased. If left alone, unhampered by regulation, the marketplace can sort out these issues, considering technical requirements, processing parameters, and economics. There is simply no way that an *a priori* political process can do as well.

Let me relate two stories that illustrate this point. First, several years ago, I visited the local Coca-Cola Bottling Company in Tampa, an organization that was recycling a number of products that were produced in the normal course of business, such as corrugated boxes, plastic film, plastic boxes, aluminum cans, and glass.

But its most ingenious recycling achievement involved water. There are a number of water uses in a typical bottling plant, ranging from the highest and best uses of treated water in the product itself to lower, less critical uses in container rinsing and soap lubricants on conveyor lines. The company was so successful in its recycling program that it was paid a visit by local water department officials. They wanted to know why its monthly bill of $50,000 per month had dropped to around $25,000. It was revealed that an ordinary mechanic's sensible idea—to create a hierarchy of water uses and to recycle— was responsible. It is a wonderful example of how knowledge of circumstance, driven by a desire to do better, yields economic efficiency and environmental protection.

The second story dates back to 1961. When I first joined the Coca-Cola Company, I visited a bottle cap manufacturing plant in Atlanta. At the end of the process, bottle caps were stamped out of a printed sheet of metal, leaving a lace-like honeycomb of residual metal. As an industrial engineer I was interested in what happened to the scrap. I asked the plant manager about how he disposed of it. He said offhandedly, "Oh, we sell it to a guy who makes furnace filters." This casual comment lay dormant in my mind for several decades, until I was exposed to government regulators who thought they could not only specify packages for everything within the economy but also make decisions about what should be done with the waste streams from manufacturing operations. Would they have ever thought of such a wonderful idea?

Price and Efficiency

Friedrich A. Hayek wrote: "The price system is just one of those formulations which man has learned to use after he had stumbled on it without understanding it." He has explained that the price mechanism is a marvel because of the information it communicated to all parties—without the parties being required to understand every aspect of creation of the product or its cost.

Many of those arguing for packaging and recycling regulations allege that we are wasting resources. But if they looked closely at how the price mechanism works, they would see that the opposite is true. The marketplace forces efficiency into the system because it rewards improved products and improved prices.

In 1961, the 12-ounce beverage can weighed 164 pounds per 1,000. Then the steel industry developed a new technology, "double-cold reduction," which reduced the weight of the steel used in each can. This new rolling technology then produced a smoother metal, which reduced the amount of tin required to cover the hills and valleys in the can's surface.

But there was still that soldered side seam, and the solder was made of an alloy of tin and lead. As a customer buying millions of cans each year, Coca-Cola did not like the soldered side seam, and we told our suppliers. So, Continental Can developed a welded side seam, and American Can developed an adhesive-bonded side seam, and the lead solder was eliminated.

Since the can was no longer soldered, there was no need for the tin—and the can industry moved away from tinplate to black plate. Then the aluminum industry decided to compete for a share of the 12-ounce beverage can market, and they produced a two-piece aluminum can. The steel industry responded with the development of a two-piece steel can, and both industries, through metallurgical innovations, design changes, and process improvements, continued to innovate and reduce the weight of their respective beverage containers.

Today, the 12-ounce aluminum beverage can weighs less than 31 pounds per 1,000, signifying reduction in weight of *over 80 percent.* If I hold a 12-ounce carbonated beverage can currently used by the soft drink and brewing industries in one hand, I can easily tear it apart with the other. I could not have done this in 1961. Competition between steel and aluminum, between glass and plastic, between cans and bottles, drove the innovation and creativity and the new capital investments that I have just described. They occurred in a market economy that forced competitors to *add value* by being innovative and, in so doing, they produced lighter-weight packages with less waste and lower environmental impact. Government regulation could never have accomplished what the market accomplished. Government regulation would have stalled innovation, fixed technology, and locked in inefficient systems, as centralized planning has done in Eastern Europe, the former Soviet Union, and everywhere it has been tried.

To explore this idea further, let us turn to another example of consumer packaging. Chances are you have seen and purchased at least one little square beverage container called a "drink box." This package is safe, lightweight, easy to handle, easy to carry, and it protects the product extremely well. It has allowed whole milk to be broadly and economically distributed throughout the Third World because it does not require refrigeration. If you should ever visit Kenya, take a look at a 10-shilling note: On the front of those issued in the 1980s there is the president's picture; on the back there are two children, two cows, and two drink boxes. It is no wonder that a few years ago, the Institute of Food Technologists voted the drink box the most important innovation in food technology of the last fifty years.

Yet not long ago, the state of Maine banned the drink box since it claimed that it is nonrecyclable. It is true that it is made from several layers of different materials, but plant scrap from the production of this form of packaging is routinely recycled. The drink box also uses less material, less energy, and produces less waste than any alternative single-serving package throughout its production and distribution. It even does better than all multi-serve alternatives, and it does not require refrigeration like many other juice packages. The drink box truly has an impeccable set of environmental credentials.

Keeping Free Enterprise Free

After nearly four years of difficult, expensive lobbying, free market environmentalists and packaging companies finally were able to get the law repealed and put drink boxes back on the market in Maine. It was one more hurdle successfully overcome in the race called American business. But was it a hurdle that needed to be there in the first place? Anyone looking at the hard facts should say "no." It is not regulation but private property rights, individual action, self-adjusting prices, and competition that forces adaptation to changing conditions and drives efficient resource utilization. In other words, free enterprise has kept us focused, fast, flexible, and competitive in a complex world market and that is the key to thriving in the future.

DAVE THOMAS

What Makes for Success?

A First Word

There are all kinds of success and all kinds of ways to achieve it. I know bus drivers who are as successful as bankers. I know anonymous computer programmers who are now more successful than some of the biggest sports celebrities. I also know glamorous Hollywood stars and leading political figures who are failures. Sometimes you can spot true success. Sometimes you can't. Success can take many forms, but one thing's for sure: There are certain ingredients that are necessary in any recipe for success, and they may be applied by anyone.

In other words, success comes through doing the right things—developing proper skills, attitudes, and values. As I've thought this through from an ordinary guy's perspective (which, above all else, I am; Lord knows, I'm no scholar), I have come to identify twelve ingredients. We know them as "character traits" or "values" or "virtues." People have been making lists of these ingredients ever since the Bible was written—and even before then. I've seen lists that are longer and some that are shorter, but twelve feels just about right to me. They are the ones that have made the most sense and have proved most valuable in my walk through life.

But I should warn you, making lists is not enough to achieve success. You have to show people what success is. For example, I don't think that we really need to define generosity; we need to show what it means to be more generous—with our time, our talents, and our treasures

My list of ingredients for success is divided into four basic groups:

1. *Inward:* These have to do with getting your own act together successfully.

2. *Outward:* These are all about treating people right.

3. *Upward:* These are skills you need to know if you want to go beyond just doing an okay job and truly excel.

4. *Onward:* These are attitudes you need to have in order to put yourself second and other people first. I think that onward values may be the toughest and the most rewarding values of all.

Added on to these ingredients are some others. Since I'm a hamburger cook, I call them "toppings." They are the pickles and onions of how I look at success:

- Anything is possible within the laws of God and man.

- You can't cut corners on quality.

- Give back—early and often.

- When you help someone, you really help yourself.

- Pay attention to the basics.

- You can't make much progress walking forward if you don't keep your balance, and that means balance in every part of your life.

- Have a sense of urgency about most things you do, and you won't end up as the caboose.

- Focus on only one thing at a time, and on just a few things in a lifetime.

- Don't waste time trying to do things you know nothing about: Either learn the basics or steer clear.

- Remember that life is short and fragile. Live it as if you don't know if you are going to be around for the next breath.

- Don't take the people of our nation—or their freedom—for granted.

- Be yourself—don't take yourself too seriously.

- Do the right thing—even when it may seem like the hardest thing in the world.

- Put more into life than you get out of it.

Inward: Getting Your Own Act Together

Success starts inside. Unless your own attitude and beliefs are right, you can never be a success. That goes for being successful in raising your family or helping to lead your church or synagogue or just making a buck. People never really have their act together unless they are honest, they believe in something, and they develop basic discipline.

Honesty

Many good people may look at honesty backwards. They think that it's okay if they don't come forward with the whole truth until someone challenges them with the right questions. But honesty doesn't mean hiding in the weeds; it means stepping out and telling the whole truth. Honesty means being sincere. It also means being fair in all your dealings with others.

Honesty is the number-one ingredient for success. I learned this the way most people do: through trial and error. I was born out of wedlock in New Jersey in 1932. A Michigan couple adopted me just after I was born. My adopted mother died when I was only five, but I had the good fortune to have a wonderful adoptive grandmother, Minnie Sinclair, who looked out for my welfare and helped shape my beliefs. I did not discover that I was adopted for many years, and, I have to admit, this made me angry and resentful for some time. I wish I had known from the beginning.

Yet after I learned the truth, I didn't always share it with others. One day, an African-American Wendy's manager buttonholed me and said, "Dave, when you gave your speech today, you left out the part about being adopted. Why did you do that? I always related to that because I was adopted myself." The comment hit home. From that point on, I made it a practice to be fully honest—and proud—about my past.

Faith

Honesty doesn't come from out of nowhere. It is a product of your moral convictions. But what do you do when your convictions are challenged? It is faith that gives you the strength to go on believing. Though I am a Christian, I respect the religions of others, and I think that they play a vital role in our society. But I don't support convictions or cults that are negative and lead only to hatred and fanaticism. Faith must be positive.

Live your faith. Don't wear it on your sleeve; roll up both sleeves and do something about it. When I was eleven years old, my adoptive grandmother took me to Michigan's Gull Lake to be baptized by immersion. I really felt that I was accepted by God when I was baptized. But what I remember most about my baptism was that my Grandma Minnie made it happen. For her, Christianity meant more than doctrine you talked about on Sundays. It meant working hard in a restaurant, seeing to the lodgers she rented rooms to, tending a big garden, doing the canning, and taking care of the farm animals every morning. And it meant teaching her grandson about faith.

At night we would listen to a gospel radio station that broadcast out of Chicago; on Sundays, before church, we would listen to shows like the Cato Tabernacle out of Indianapolis. The public praying and singing part of her faith might not have stuck with me all that much, but I got baptized into the roll-up-your-sleeves kind of faith of Grandma Minnie. And I believe in it to this day.

Discipline

Routine lies at the heart of discipline. Routine is what keeps us focused on the main things in life. But routine doesn't have to mean boring. Unless you have a strong, healthy routine, I doubt that you can live a successful life. Discipline means keeping things and people in their proper places. For example, I think that taxpayers should discipline their politicians so that they don't get too uppity! Children need discipline, too—plenty more than most of them get—and that's the fault of their parents. Discipline means direction—clear and firm direction—not physical or mental abuse. Discipline helps you keep track of your own thinking and also keeps such thinking simple and to the point so that you don't mess up by dreaming up fancy, big-shot thoughts when you shouldn't.

Roy Tuggle, one of the pioneers of the modern restaurant business, is a classic in discipline as far as I'm concerned. When he was fourteen years old, Roy—the sixth of twelve children—left Ravenna, Kentucky, during the Great Depression. With only two years of school under his belt, nine pennies in his pocket, and cardboard soles in his shoes, he hopped a freight train to Columbus, Ohio. After unloading stoves and refrigerators and working as a dishwasher, he became a fry cook. By sheer will and discipline he built his career and a great restaurant business while he and his wife Mary raised their family.

When Roy started out, hamburgers were only a nickel and a small restaurant operator had to scrimp for every penny. Years later, when Roy sold his business, he became a millionaire. But the dollar signs never changed Roy. He's never been driven by money. As you'll hear Roy often put it today, "I never wanted to be the richest man in the graveyard," to which I'll generally chime in, "You got it, Roy. You've never seen a hearse with luggage racks." Roy's is the kind of discipline that keeps success from going to your head once you have had the good fortune to achieve your goals.

Outward: Treating People Right

Success may start inside, but it doesn't mean anything until you draw other people into the picture. The key is whether you are going to be fair to other folks—will you treat people right? If you are to treat people right, you have to master three fundamentals: caring, teamwork, and support. Most of us are lucky enough to learn these basic ideas from our parents and should be pros at them by the time we are in nursery school. (But I have met some Ph.D.s and millionaires who have never learned the words or have forgotten what they mean, and I bet that you know people like that, too.) Not taking people for granted is a great way to steer a straight outward course and to do right by your fellow human beings.

Caring

Caring is the rock that love is built upon. Caring is feeling what another person feels. Some people call it "empathy." Genuinely caring about people usually leads to success. And really successful people widen the circle of people they care about more and more as they grow older. Mary Kay Ash, founder of Mary Kay Cosmetics, once told me something I'll never forget. She said the one suggestion she got in life that helped her most was to "pretend that every single person you meet has a sign around his or her neck that says, 'Make me feel important.'"

Why aren't we just nice to people? One year, shortly before Christmas, I went to a Wendy's restaurant in Albuquerque to film a television program about adoption with two youngsters. The little girl, who was about seven, had a fresh scar where her father had walloped her with a beer bottle. That scar wasn't going to go away. As we ate lunch along with a friend of mine, the girl and her older brother, who was about nine, finally started to look us in the eyes, and that was none too easy for them. We talked about how important it is to stick together when you don't have other family. And then the boy said: "I don't want to be adopted with her. Just look at her ugly scar!"

It may seem cruel, but he was right. The boy knew his sister's appearance would turn off many possible adoptive parents. And before you condemn him, think back for a minute: Were you any less selfish when you were nine? I doubt that I was. My friend—who is smart in a low-key way and who made it big-time by building a big business over the years—reached into his wallet and pulled out two crisp one hundred dollar bills. "You kids," he said in a real quiet voice, "don't have any money to buy Christmas presents. It's plain to see that. So I want you to buy some Christmas presents, but there's a catch. You can't buy anything for yourself. Think hard about what your brother or sister might like or need and buy that instead. Finally, you have to write me a letter about what you got each other."

That five-minute course in caring outdid the best universities anywhere. The brother and sister made up. In January, my friend received a letter reporting what they bought each other, and he sent a copy to me. Then we learned that they had been adopted by a family. As I hear it, they're quite a team, and their new parents are proud to have them—because of the way that they care for each other and for lots of other reasons, too.

Teamwork

Teamwork is the starting point for treating people right. Most people think that teamwork is only important when competing against other teams. But competition is only part of the picture. In most things we do in life, people have to work with rather than against each other to get something done. Win-win situations and partnerships are the most important results of teamwork. The best teams in the world are the ones that help people become better and achieve more than they ever thought they could on their own.

One place people learn teamwork is from their families. Children get their first lesson watching how their parents behave toward each other. So, if you're a parent, you are also a teacher of teamwork—for good or ill—every day. Your sons and daughters learn from what you do. For me, the people I've worked with have become my family, too. Throughout my career, my "second family" has taught me a whole lot about teamwork.

There are little teams and there are big teams. Your community is a team, for example. My daughter Pam organizes volunteer work for the city of Columbus, so she knows a lot about how to get different kinds of teams to work together, on projects ranging from recreation centers to hospital boards. Teams can work together, and teams can compete, too, even when they are not rivals. Why aren't Pam's kids jealous when she spends so much of her time on community work? There is a simple answer: The kids are all involved in community work themselves, and they have been from an early age. Pam and her husband, Steve, endorse it and encourage it. The community team isn't a rival or an opponent of the family team—it's an extension of it. Neat idea, don't you think?

Support

Many people believe that support is something you give to someone you feel sorry for or that it means propping someone up who would fail unless you were there to give him a boost. But that's not the way I see it. Support is the boost you give someone who can help himself but who needs a partner to open a window or to push aside a roadblock. Support isn't a bunch of reckless advice, either. It's real help—commitment and effort. Support is "teamwork plus." Support is also sharing feelings and insights with other people. It's helping others with their level of awareness and making your own awareness stronger at the same time.

The best way to get support is to give it. Wendy's President Gordon Teter likes to remind people of a saying that Jack Mollenkopf, his college coach at Purdue, often used: "Meet me halfway, and it's amazing what can happen." It is amazing what can be done when you treat people with respect. Respect goes both ways, too. Just as the players need it from the coach, the coach needs it from the players.

Support is also easier if things aren't too complicated. Gordon believes in what he calls "The Law of the Lowest Common Denominator," and it has nothing to do with arithmetic. It goes like this: "The simpler you can keep it, the better you can execute it." It's that way for a department and its boss, for a congregation and its minister, and for a volunteer group and its chairperson. If you want to give and get support, it's a lot more likely to come and keep coming if the rules are simple and clear.

Upward: Going for Excellence and Beyond

When you have your own act together and get along well with others, you're ready to reach for another goal, that of excellence. Nothing is as tricky in the world of success as excellence. From our earliest days, we are taught that it is snazzy, glossy, bigger than life. It's that three seconds of glory when a major leaguer puts one out of the park or a figure skater completes a triple jump, not the constant training or workouts. But that's just false. Most people think excellence in business is sitting at a big desk and making power decisions, but true excellence is really the years beforehand making little and big decisions and learning from mistakes when things go wrong.

No one can excel in everything. In fact, excellence in any one little thing is hard enough. And don't forget: It's easy to become selfish when you "go for the gold." The graveyards of the world are loaded with people who lost it all at the same time they thought they were winning it all.

Motivation

Without a doubt, motivation is a key ingredient of success. Know what motivates you, and prove to yourself that this motivation is honest and worthwhile. But don't let too many different things motivate you, or you'll be tangled up in a maze of all kinds of conflicts. Stay focused. Figure out what your motivations are going to be in the next step of your life before you arrive at it. Keep dreaming, but don't daydream. And don't do anything just to earn praise, or you are likely to shortchange yourself in the end. Look at success firsthand so that you really know how it works and what it costs to achieve.

It may be corny, but I'm big on lapel pins. Some people hand out business cards; I give away lapel pins. Wendy's gives out pins to employees, and to customers, too—they're just as much a part of the family as anyone else. As I said, I don't believe in wearing your beliefs on your sleeve; but I do believe in wearing them on your lapel. Yep, I'm one of those guys who'll wear an American flag pin on my lapel from time to time; it shows I'm proud to be an American. In the same way, by wearing Wendy's lapel pins, our employees show they're proud to be a part of the Wendy's team. Does having a little symbol that means they're part of the Wendy's family motivate employees to work a little harder, or customers to come in more often? A little bit, I'll bet. And success in life is made up of a lot of little things that keep you motivated and that motivate others too.

Creativity

Creativity means change, but if you don't use common sense when you change things around, you are likely to end up farther behind than when you started. Not everybody can be creative. Accept it as a fact of life that if you aren't creative yourself your challenge is to learn how to work with people who are. And being creative doesn't always mean doing new things. Sometimes, it's using a creative idea that worked in one instance and applying it to another. I'm a disciple of reality. Successful creative dreams have to be realistic—within man's laws as well as God's—and within the realm of common sense.

What makes people creative? Sometimes, it's having your life shaken up. George Valassis is a pal of mine. For nineteen years he worked as an advertising salesman for his father's brother. One day his uncle decided to retire and his cousin took over the business. The cousin fired him. Without warning, George lost a modest though comfortable job, and he realized then and there that job security could vanish like a puff of smoke. So, he put his nineteen years of experience to use in order to come up with an innovative idea. He knew that advertisers like Procter and Gamble and General Foods were having a really tough time delivering coupons to customers quickly, so he came up with the idea of inserting books filled with coupons in newspapers. To this day, when you open the Sunday edition of your newspaper and see a book of coupons inside, you're looking at what the ad industry calls a "Valassis Insert." George sold the company he built for big bucks. If he hadn't gotten fired, would he have come up with this great idea? George doesn't think so. He says he just played the hand he was dealt. Pretty creative though, wasn't it?

Leadership

Everybody is saying that we need to stop putting leaders on pedestals. I'm not so sure. The real problem is finding leaders who truly deserve to keep their pedestals. What knocks off more leaders than anything else is failing to practice what they preach. Of all the things leaders are supposed to do, nothing is more important than setting a good example. Ben Franklin had it right when he wrote in *Poor Richard's Almanac*, "Well done is better than well said." I don't think we should do away with pedestals; we ought to be putting a lot more "little people"—people who have really achieved something—on them so that ordinary folks have a better, clearer idea of who's doing the job and who's setting the pace.

J. B. Fuqua is a titan of industry who built a huge conglomerate and broadcast empire. J. B. is also a guy who still knows the meaning of being humble. Born to a poor family, his mother died when he was two months old, and his grandparents adopted him. When J. B. was out on his own and wanted to learn about radio electronics, the only library he knew about was Duke University's. The library staff decided to loan him the books he needed even though he was not a student. It wasn't a bad deal for Duke: After J. B. hit the bull's-eye in his own companies, he invested $15 million in the Duke University business school, helping to put it in the front ranks of all business schools in the U.S.

First and foremost, J. B. is a leader. In addition to the donations he's made to Duke, he's donated $4 million to train managers in Russia and Ukraine as these nations attempt to put at least a few true free enterprise principles into practice. And then there's the $10 million that he's giving to Prince Edward County, Virginia, to help turn around the educational system for youngsters in kindergarten through twelfth grade. It will be a model of doing the right thing for rural school systems throughout the United States.

It's not the money that makes J. B. successful as a leader. It's the fact that he won't let go. J. B. will tell you that leadership doesn't stop with giving but begins there. He's well past retirement age, yet you'll find him all over—from Farmville to Kiev—giving to others, passing on his own experience and wisdom. J. B.'s style is real leadership—letting go in the doing, but not letting go in the guiding.

Onward: Putting Yourself Second and Others First

If going upward and reaching for excellence is where success gets tricky, going onward by putting yourself second and others first is where success really gets tough. Most books on success tell you that you have really "arrived" when you win the race. That's wrong. Truly successful people are the ones who help others cross the finish line. People who make this last big step toward success really have three things: responsibility, courage, and generosity. Onward is the direction Success Soldiers follow—Christian or any other kind.

Responsibility

We try to teach children responsibility and that's good, but, as I have already said, most of us don't learn the full meaning of responsibility until we are older and have gained solid experience, made some decisions, and learned from our mistakes—not the simple mistakes we make when "following orders," but mistakes we make when trying to do something really hard or trying to excel. Making these sorts of mistakes teaches us judgment, and it helps toughen our backbone.

Mature responsibility means realizing that no single person can be responsible for everything. You can't be successful if you are stumbling around trying to juggle the whole world on your shoulders. Responsible people refuse to take shortcuts, even though they are almost always available. They make sure that others with duties act responsibly, too. And they use whatever recognition or honor they may have earned not to further their own ends but on behalf of good causes. Instead of stealing the limelight, they allow it to shine upon a good cause.

My son Kenny says that the most important piece of advice I ever gave him came in 1979 as the two of us were driving over the Oakland Park Bridge in Ft. Lauderdale. He was thinking about becoming a Wendy's franchisee. I gave him my opinion: I was against it. I didn't come out and say why, but my feeling was that he wasn't ready for that kind of responsibility, and I didn't want to see him fail. When he told me his mind was made up, I said, "Don't ever forget how you got here, and don't ever let yourself become complacent." Kenny went on to become pretty successful in the restaurant business. He says my advice really helped him. But I could have summed up everything I said that day in just two words: Be responsible.

Courage

We tend to make courage too dramatic. Courage is often doing something simple, unpleasant, or boring again and again until we get it down pat. People who are physically challenged and who have the determination to get around their handicaps are great examples because their courage makes them test their limits every day in a way that the rest of us write off as small-time or insignificant. Lois Gruenbaum grew up in Cleveland and went to work in a hospital kitchen when she was fifteen. During World War II, she became a nurse's aide and worked in an army hospital. After a shift, she would say to herself, "Hey, things are bad, but there's always someone who is worse off. All you need to do is find out what you can and can't do and then go ahead and do what you can do."

Great lesson—Lois learned it not long before she needed to put it to use. In 1955, she was diagnosed with cancer. Operation after operation followed, but the cancer always came back. Finally, she lost one leg and half of the pelvic bone and was forced to drag herself around on crutches. She came home from the hospital faced with the challenge of taking care of her husband, a seven-year-old, a four-year-old, and two-year-old twins. She says she cut a deal with the Lord: "I promised that if He let me live to raise my children, I would not vegetate. I would be a contributing person." It was a good deal. Forty years later, the family is flourishing, and Lois is one of the most active and happy people you could ever hope to meet. And there are thousands of such quiet, unsung heroes in every town. I'll bet you know lots of people with the courage of Lois Gruenbaum.

Generosity

A person who has modest means and won't share may be considered stingy. But rich people can give 'til they're purple and still not be truly generous. You have to give of yourself, not just of your wallet. One of the things I'm proudest about in the Wendy's family is that so many franchisees make significant donations to the community—and they contribute leadership as well as dollars. Another old friend, the late Kenny King, was a generous guy who had a real knack for how he gave. He really took pleasure in it, was modest about it, and often gave anonymously. But even more important was the fact that he really tried to learn what giving was all about. Whether he was giving people moral or financial support, he would always say, "I'm really getting a lot more out of this than you are." I can't tell you how many times he said that same thing to me. Later, when I tried to do for others what Kenny had done for me, I learned what he meant. When you give people help and understanding, you truly learn what they are like. And those who understand others better are certainly the most likely to succeed. The giving and the getting become all mixed up—which is great.

The Proud Beggar

In February of 1991, I had to travel to Memphis. It wasn't a trip I wanted to make. There's a church there I'll never forget; you don't forget places where you say good-bye to your best

friends. It's plenty bigger than Calvary Church in Kalama-
zoo where I had my first memories of going to church. In
fact, it's a cathedral—the Cathedral of the Immaculate Conception. It looks Spanish and it's mighty big and fancy. On the
day I was there, every seat was filled, and a huge crowd stood
outside. A lot of other people—not just me—had lost a friend.

> Oh, Danny boy, the pipes, the pipes are calling,
> From glen to glen and down the mountainside,
> The summer's gone—all the roses falling,
> 'Tis you, 'tis you must go, and I must bide.

A song you'd expect to hear in an Irish pub, not in a cathedral. You wouldn't expect it to be sung by a Metropolitan Opera soprano like Marguerite Piazza either. Maybe you'd think
that it was honoring an Irish cardinal, but who would expect
that it was in memory of a Lebanese entertainer of humble
origins? Many eyes were tearing before the music started, but
when they heard the first notes of that song—Danny Thomas's
theme song for decades—everybody choked up. A little girl
and an older couple near me were crying, and I don't know
what sound seemed bigger to my ears—the crying or the music.

Danny was a great friend. He was one heck of a showman.
But, most of all, he was a success—not just as an entertainer
but as a human being. An obsession drove him—the St. Jude's
Children's Hospital in Memphis. He'd do anything for that
hospital. No man or woman I know ever got over every inch
of the false pride that we are all born with more than Danny
Thomas did. He called himself the "Proud Beggar."

If Danny Thomas hadn't forgotten a promise, St. Jude would
never have been built. Back in 1943, Danny was still playing
five-dollar-a-week gigs. His wife was pregnant with their first
child, Marlo, and they needed money to raise a family. Danny's
uncle by marriage was a butcher who offered him a job cutting meat, but he wanted to stay in show business. Danny stopped at a church and, according to the Catholic tradition, prayed
to St. Jude for direction. He promised he would show his grati-

tude if guided to the right path: Should he be a comedian or a butcher? Not much later, Danny's act was booked at Chez Paris in Chicago. He had made it to the big time. The booking lasted for five years, and it helped launch his television career.

Until well into his stint at Chez Paris, Danny had forgotten all about his promise. Forgetting to make good on a promise was about the worst thing a person could do in Danny's book. When he finally remembered, he went to see an old friend, Cardinal Stritch, and he asked what he should do. The cardinal told him that there were already enough churches and enough statues in the world. Recalling his first parish in Memphis, he proposed the idea of starting a children's hospital there.

That's what Danny did. He built the best children's hospital in the world. Why is the place named after St. Jude? St. Jude is the saint in charge of impossible acts. Danny felt that "no child should die in the dawn of life," so he declared a personal war against the killer diseases that strike the young. He started funding the hospital in Memphis in 1957. Great names in medicine led the research. Plenty of impossible things were made possible because Danny stuck to his mission like a bulldog. In 1962, only 4 percent of the victims of acute lymphocytic leukemia survived the disease; in 1991, 73 percent survived. Only 7 percent of patients with non-Hodgkin's lymphoma recovered; now, about 80 percent do. The list goes on and on. When people tell you about the "impossible," just think of St. Jude's Hospital.

In 1991, Danny Thomas was promoting his new book, the proceeds of which were earmarked for St. Jude. He always did fund-raising for the hospital before taking on jobs that would put money in his own pocket. One night, worn out, he got home late. At 2:30 a.m., a massive heart attack killed him. He was not buried in some grassy cemetery. He was laid to rest in a mausoleum inside St. Jude's Hospital. All around the mausoleum, Danny's favorite sayings are inscribed—sayings like:

"Blessed is the man who knows why he was born," and "He who denies his heritage has no heritage." Danny gave of himself. He taught others to give of themselves, too, and to forget their selfish side. I remember his response to a donor who had put down a large hunk of change: "The deepest thank-you I can offer is to pray that you and yours will never need the help of St. Jude's."

Well done, Danny boy!

Danny Thomas's example is worth remembering anytime the temptation arises for "me" to take over "we." Everything that made him a success was based on simple principles:

- Keep your word. Danny kept his word to God.

- Let a good cause that's bigger than you take over your life. What is your St. Jude? There ought to be one. Think about it, and support it.

- Don't get scared by the word impossible. In fact, get together the best talents you can find to tackle the impossible.

- Do it through people. Danny got people to work together. That's the way it should be, isn't it?

Whether you are passing the hat for a good cause, defending your beliefs, teaching your children, helping your community, or starting a business, be a proud beggar. Real proud.

Victor Niederhoffer

Music, Counting, and Speculation: What Entrepreneurs Need to Know About the Market

Everywhere my father Artie went there was music. He heard music as he stepped through life; he hummed it on the street, danced to it on the beach, played it on the violin in the house. When I asked him as a kid why he was always making music, he had a simple answer: "Because I'm happy." Then he'd say, "It makes man great."

The tune Artie liked best was the theme from the Third Movement of Schubert's Quintet in A Major ("The Trout") for piano and string. The melody opens like most great violin concertos, with a simple D major chord and then moves to a falling scale over the dominant A major harmony. The pure happiness, the images of a birds singing and a bubbling brook full of trout easily escaping the fishermen, that this simple melody evokes are beyond description in mere words. Many musicians have wanted this song played as an epitaph at their funeral. My father, who was policeman by profession and a musician by vocation, unfortunately, had his wish fulfilled at the prime

The author wishes to acknowledge the assistance of and thank Robert Schrade, Roy Niederhoffer, and Paul Buethe, three eminent musicians and speculators who made valuable contributions to this essay, which is excerpted from *The Education of a Speculator* (Wiley, forthcoming).

of his life, at the age of 63. The family violin teacher, Gregory Zartsky, played it.

How the Market Moves

When the markets are moving in my favor in a nice gentle way, I often think of the trout quintet. We have a piano in the office. If the felicitous moves repeat often enough, one of the professional musicians who seems to gravitate to my employ is sure to dash out a few variations of "The Trout." If we happen to be making money for or doing business for the famous financier and investor George Soros, the variation preferred is the rapid Fourth Movement, a beautiful rondo in the Hungarian style.

I never thought that I would have a kind word to say about the mystics in my field who draw lines between two or three random low points and high points in a chart and then compute a percent. Gann, Elliot, and Fibonnocci analysis are a few of the names they utter to gain that appeal to authority that invariably litters this type of pseudo-science. But I have taken to drawing a five-line treble clef around the price movements of markets during a day or week. Often I hear the prices sounding out a tune in A major key if going up, or A minor key if going down. Artie had a book, *Dictionary of Musical Melodies*, that he often consulted when he heard a tune on the radio; it enables one to find out from a theme transposed in C what the piece is that contained it. I use this book sometimes to figure out the music I am looking at in the charts. But I have not quantified whether the final resting place can be figured out from the opening of them. At first, my colleagues laughed at me when I sat them down to see the similarities between music and the market. But now, at the end of each day, one of them is sure to say, "It can't go down any more. It ended on the diminished 7th chord."

Another frequent work I hear in the market is Symphony no. 94, "The Surprise." "The Surprise" is a simple fortissimo chord in the second movement, designed "to make the women jump." In a review of this piece, a lyrical critic for *The Oracle* wrote, "'The Surprise' might be likened to the situation of a beautiful Shepherdess who, lulled to sleep by the murmur of a distant Waterfall, starts, alarmed by the unexpected firing of a fowling-piece." Right after lunch time or before a holiday, the markets have a tendency to meander up and down in a five-point range similar to the twinkle, twinkle-like simple C major fifths of this symphony. Often, a startling move is imminent; be sure not to be lulled to sleep by the murmuring of water, or worse yet, thoughts of a beautiful, slumbering shepherdess.

Near the end of Artie's life when he was struggling with cancer, he was more likely to hum the "Passacalia" of Handel in G minor. "It makes life endurable," he would mutter if someone asked. Pieces in a minor key often evoke tragic emotions in Western listeners. When the market is in the process of destroying us, someone in our office is likely to play the "Funeral March" of the Third Symphony of Beethoven in C minor. When the oboes come in announcing the procession of pallbearers, someone in the office invariably mutters dolefully, "Oh, the bonds," or "Oh, the yen." The subsequent drum rolls imitated by the violins make me want to cry about the heroic loss that my wealth has suffered.

The Power of Music

Music has the power to bring out different emotions arising from the deepest experiences of the listener. Some fill me with power, or perhaps daydreams of infinite pleasure, or more likely, if the markets are moving against me, with tragedy. I have unfortunately not reached the sublime heights envisioned by Beethoven for "He who truly understands my music must then go free of all the misery which others bear about with them." But sometimes, at least, I imitate the Maestro's conducting style during the trading day.

While all agree that music is the universal language, or the language of the emotions, there has never been a satisfactory definition of the expressive quality of music. In 1939, American composer Aaron Copland put the problem this way: "Is there a meaning to music? My answer to that would be 'Yes,' and 'Can you state in so many words what the meaning is?' My answer to that would be 'No.'"

Music arises from the most basic impulses of humans. The vocal chords make sounds, the body and feet make rhythmic movements, and the mind transforms these sounds and movements into music. In the *Enjoyment of Music*, Machlis says it perfectly:

> [Music] has retained its connection with the springs of human feeling, with the accents of joy and sorrow, tension and release. Its procedures have been shaped by thousands of years of human experience; its expressive content mirrors man's existence, his place in nature and in society.

Western and Eastern Music

The basic texture of early Western music stems from point-counterpoint (or note against note) which is a highly developed art with many compositional rules resulting in the great Baroque master works. One key step in its development stems from the invention of musical notation. Paul Griffith and Roland DeCande make this point nicely in *The Heritage of Music*:

> The particular glory of Western classical music is its heritage . . . which is possible because it has a means of record: it has notation. . . . In Western classical music, however, the model is that of the novel, with emphasis on that is now and what has never been expressed before. . . . Nevertheless, it remains broadly true that the essence of non-western music is continuity whereas that of western music is change.

Eastern markets also show much more continuity than the Western ones. I frequently make money by playing the Hong

Kong or Indian stock market to continue their trends after a big move (with certain subtle adjustments). The serial correlation of one-day changes in the Bolsa, the Indian Stock market index, during 1994 to 1996 was 0.13, a figure significantly higher than the 0.05 for the S&P during this time period.

The most common form for almost all Western music is called the A–B–A form—statement, departure, return. The two A's help you remember the melodies: The B provides contrast. I also find this form predominating in the market. The beginning of a day is marked by up moves in one segment of the market and down moves in another. After a period of transition, the moves in the segments are reversed. Finally, the opening theme is repeated, usually with vigor in the coda at the close. Just to keep the audience in suspension, however, there are many deceptive cadences thrown in along the way. And just before the close, the entire contrasting themes are often recapitulated. Ontogeny recapitulates phylogeny in the original key. The final irony with market music is that the contrasting theme wins out often enough to prevent you from making too much money by betting on the A–B–A form. One of the musicians who works for me says it is more like a jazz piece when you know all the players and know the rhythm, but you can't predict where the opening theme will be resolved.

Mastering Music

I was very fortunate to be forced to train as a musician from the age of three. I learned with a portable paper colored keyboard that covered the piano and was synchronized with colored notes. It worked for me. By the time I was five, I had perfect pitch and could sight-read any piece as well as I can play it today. At seven, I could play the notes of the Bach three-part inventions and the Beethoven Sonatas. At nine, I could play the Mozart clarinet concerto, at the "B" level, without any lapses in fingering. Unfortunately, I preferred to hustle pennies and nickels in money games at the beach to practicing my instruments. But fortunately, my parent wouldn't allow that. Each day, seven days a week, my father sat down at the piano and forced me to play. If I claimed my clarinet was broken, he'd take out a screw driver and fix it. If while he tried to fix it, I'd try to sneak away to the beach, he'd catch me and drag me back to the bench. If I refused to practice my piano scales, my Czerny, Hanon & Beringer, he'd sit there just waiting to grab me if I tried to run away.

The cliché holds that parents often repeat the virtues and mistakes of their own upbringing. Thirty years after my dad dragged me back, my first daughter Galt refused to take her piano lesson. While her piano teacher, Robert Schrade, a gentleman I revere as the embodiment of Bach in our age waited at the piano, I tried to unobtrusively pull Galt toward the piano. I grabbed one arm: "You have to take your lesson." My wife grabbed the other: "You can't force her. You'll make her hate it." Galt at this time let me know that unless I let her go, she'd report me to the Family Abuse Authority and have me locked up. Between us, we almost pulled both of her arms out of their sockets, all the while trying to hide the donnybrook from Schrade. He started to play a transcription of a Strauss Waltz. It broke the stalemate. I won the tug of war. Amid her muffled sobs, I escorted her to the piano as if I had no care in the world. I told him later, "it was the most embarrassing moment of my life." He said that he just thought of the unbroken circles of father and daughters that had provoked similar scenes from time immemorial. I still don't know whether I did the right thing. Since that time, I've related the story and many dozens of adults have told me they wish their father had forced them when they had a similar scene. On the other hand, Galt now plays the drums, not the piano, even though she was referred to in her youth in the modern euphemism as "highly gifted at all keyboard instruments."

The training I received in practicing music every day has been the key to my success in all my subsequent activities, including speculation. I believe that the explanation is more than chance and happenstance. Music is a miracle stolen from the gods. But for humans, it's also the most natural thing in the world. There are different theories of music's origin from the songs of birds, the melodies of speech, the sounds of the battle or the hunt. It undoubtedly arose near the beginning of man's tenure on earth. It is my belief that the training methods for musicians have advanced the competence and brilliance of its performance and composers far beyond that achieved in any other field. By borrowing from the training techniques of the musician, the prospective masterer of any other elemental life-sustaining activity, such as speculation, for example, can walk with the gods and stand with the giants.

The corresponding rules for speculators are given in parentheses:

Mastering the Market or Any Elemental Activity

1. Allow no day to pass without practicing with your instrument. (Study the market every day.)

2. Get to know how your equipment is made and how it performs under all weather conditions. (Visit the exchanges and learn how to program in an assembly language.)

3. Start each day of practice by playing a single tone with varying degrees of touch and dynamic quality. (Start with the stock market first.)

4. Play one hand at a time where required by technical difficulty. (One position is enough.)

5. Never fool around, even when no one is listening. Perfect practice makes perfect performance. (Do not boast or tell friends how great your system is or throw a few contracts on "just for fun.")

6. Whenever you make a mistake, go back and repeat the passage correctly when no one is around. (Keep a record of all your losing trades.)

7. Master all the technical aspects of your play and get in condition months before your performance. Then when

you perform or compete, you will be able to concentrate on the intellectual and refined aspects. It is the shading and dynamics that create great performances. (Paper trade before you start. Save up adequate capital.)

8. Play from memory. You can't soar when you're looking at a transcript. But take notes and keep a diary of all the pluses and minuses after you play. (Calculators or computers should not be consulted during the trading day.)

9. Get into the performance hall an hour in advance and acclimate yourself to the environment. Don't talk to anyone or shake any hands before or during your performance. (Get to work by 7:10 a.m., not 8:10 a.m., just ten minutes before the markets open.)

10. Study the most elemental pieces and decisions from the standpoint of an expert. You will be astonished at how difficult it is to play a Czerny or even a Clement Sonatina perfectly. (How would George Soros have traded that one lot?)

11. Don't become stale trying to overcome the difficulties of a piece. Come back after a breather and approach it from the beginning as if you didn't know it. (Take a break when you are losing.)

12. Cultivate and nurture all emotions during practice. Open the flood gates during performance. But restrain ostentatious visible emotions when performing. (No "high fives," crying, making up alibis, or bemoaning missed trades during the trading day.)

13. Surround yourself with great masters of your art. Attend their performances. Study their books. And pay up for their lessons. (There are, for example, at least four books by George Soros and three about him available.)

Music and Counting

Music and counting are often inseparable. Gottfried Liebwitz, co-inventor of calculus, said, "Music is the pleasure the human soul experiences from counting without being aware it is counting." The thought is a variant of the Pythagorean number mysticism. The Pythagoreans discovered that the longer the vibrating string, the lower the musical note produced. Moreover, they noticed that when the lengths of the strings are exact ratios of whole numbers, of exact 2 to 3 (a fifth), 3 to 4 (a fourth), the tones will be harmonious. Yes, but, as anyone exposed to the grotesque sound of a synthesizer can attest, the frequency of vibrations of a musical note are as small a part of music as the palette of colors and paint brush are to a work of fine art. My late friend Jack Koopman, the leading eye of the antique silver industry in the 1980s and 1990s, gave me a variation of this rule when I asked him if a recent fall in the price of silver would depress the price of the fine presentation museum quality pieces he was selling: "Victor, the price of silver has as small an influence on these pieces as the price of plywood has on the fine Chippendale chest you see there."

The German poet, Heinrich Heine, expressed what seems to me to be the definitive thought on this subject:

> Nothing is more futile than theorizing about music. No doubt there are laws, mathematically strict laws, but laws are not music; they are only its conditions—just as the art of drawing and the theory of colors, or even the brush is revelation; it does not admit of exact reckoning, and the true criticism of music remains an empirical art.

Arthur Schnabel, the great mid-20th century pianist, thought the essence had to do with silence rather than with sound. He said, "Anyone can play the notes, but it's the silence in between the notes where lies the real art." If the reader will substitute the concept "speculation" or "economics" for music in the above quotes, he'll be closer to the road to riches and knowledge than if he were to read all 100,000 volumes in the Brown Mathematics Library. However, anyone who has looked at the mathematical proof of a theorem—using letters and algebraic symbols as raw material—and compared that process to composing a musical piece—using as raw material symbols for notes and instruments—knows that the activities are identical twins. That is why IBM in its heyday recruited musicians from all the good schools to find programming talent. And why almost all the speculators at my firm have been, are, or could be after the fall professional musicians.

Counting is a basic activity that is as old as the human race. Since numerous animal species, including the crow and a few plants (such as the Venus Flytrap) do it, we may consider its origin as prehistoric. Since counting preceded writing, its first purpose must be speculative. The best guess of mathematicians is that it sprang from the human need to record or transmit information about some goods desired, hunted, owned, or stolen. The fingers and feet were good up to a certain quantity and are still used today for that purpose. But for larger numbers, stones, bones, and shells proved more practical.

But these were too ephemeral for memorializing and preserving important transactions. This led at an early stage to the cutting of notches in bones or sticks. The use of sticks to evidence debts, licenses, and payments to warriors (and their families) who recently conquered territories eventually led to a market in such sticks. And from this humble beginning, our word and market for stocks developed. The other field of counting, that of geometry, also sprang from the practical affairs of goods. The Egyptians noticed that the Nile flooded their lands each year. They needed to plant and recalculate boundaries based on the extent of the flooding and to figure out when to plant and harvest.

Counting, like music and speculation, may be thought of as mirroring the human experience and place in nature. That to me is why you can't have one without the other. Yet everyone is a mathematician. When you buy or sell something in a market, hang wallpaper or a picture, decorate or dance, you are exercising the mathematical faculty. Unfortunately, opening any psychology text will readily remind us that our senses deceive us too often to rely on general impression. Try looking at the moon when it is on the horizon versus directly over head to refresh yourself about all the illusions we are subject to. Or better yet, try to count something without benefit of mechanical checks to see how variable the process is even when your senses don't deceive.

One of the people who taught me about the importance of counting was Artie. One beautiful summer day when I was seven, I was stunned by the sacrilegious sight of my dad making marks on a big yellow pad while he was watching the best handball players in the world compete at Garber Stadium. After each point I saw the notations: OTWK—off the wall killer; KW—killer, winner; DW—drive winner; DE—drive error; A—ace; AW—angle winner. He was calculating the chances of winning the next point after runs of winning and losing points of different magnitudes. He also recorded the duration of each point, and the percentage of winners and errors for each game, contingent on various leads.

"Why are you doing that, Dad?" I asked. "Who cares when you get the points as long as you know who's best?"

"Did you ever notice how Moey Orenstein, the greatest doubles player ever, usually gets behind, 15-11 and then goes on to win, 21-19?"

"Everyone knows that. He gets behind early so he can take in more bets at better odds when he's behind. Then he comes in with his patented overhand, off the wall dead killers, hit with backspin."

"That's right," my dad said. "But notice how when he's playing a tournament match or a non-betting trophy match, like the match he played against Vic for the unofficial world title, he doesn't get behind ever."

On October 20, 1987, after the stock market crash had sent the Dow down 500 points the previous day, the market opened with a few short up ticks from follow-up buying based on the overnight rise in bond prices. But then the liquidation started again, in wild abandon. Finally, the tension became so unbearable that the trading had to be stopped on all markets except the Chicago Board of Trade Major Market Index. The silence was dynamic. I was reminded most of all of the Fifth Symphony. It is a victory symphony, with a path from strife to triumph, ending with C major chords played by thundering trombones, contrabassoons, and shrilling piccolos, a hurricane of bullishness. "But the goblins were there," as E. M. Forster says in *Howard's End*, and he adds, "They could return." By the end of trading on October 20, the Dow had risen 200 points, half the previous day's carnage, and the seeds had been planted for the greatest bull market in history, encompassing a tripling in the next nine years. But not without a few goblins returning, for example, on Thursday morning, October 20, when the averages opened below the old lows.

Music was never the same after the Fifth Symphony. Nor would markets ever be the same after the October 1987 stock crash or the COMEX silver crash of February 1980. After the latter, I asked Artie to spend a day with me at the COMEX to see the transformation. I told him that there was music, beautiful and horrible, in the market just the same as in the singing of birds or the baying of hounds chasing game. "The visit to the pits will expose you to a crowd that can't be missed in a lifetime," I coaxed. He agreed to come and I escorted him onto the trading floor at the World Trade Center.

While Artie watched the market gyrate up and down as hundreds of floor traders fought like vipers in a battle reliving the 1979-1980 rise from $5 to $50 and back to $10 again in every 15-minute interval, I received a call on my beeper. One of my clients—my major client—needed my help in launching a bear raid on the entire stock markets of the world. My head started spinning.

I called Artie up the next day for a bit of Monday morning quarterbacking. "Wasn't that amazing? Did I exaggerate when I said it was the most exciting music you'll ever hear?"

He was reticent. Finally he said, "These powerful forces, they're like an avalanche. How can you withstand them?" Like the old cop that he was, he added, "Remember those bodies of big shot speculators I have to deliver to the morgue? You're in over your head."

"Don't worry, Dad" I replied, "There's no danger. I have it all quantified."

JOHN ENGLER

The Michigan Miracle: A Model for the 21st Century

Ideas in Action

"It's the economy, stupid." The slogan is as fresh today as it was during the presidential campaign four years ago that cost Republicans the White House. Why? Because, despite White House press releases to the contrary, the performance of the American economy in the 1990s continues to be of concern. The U.S. Commerce Department reports that the nation's gross domestic product (GDP) expanded by only 2.3 percent in the first quarter of 1996. Stephen Moore of the Cato Institute observes that if the GDP sputters ahead at this pace through the year 2000—which is what most economists are forecasting—then the 1990s will go down as the century's second poorest decade for economic growth and income growth. Only the 1930s were worse.

Further, the American middle class is feeling the pinch. According to the Bureau of Labor Statistics, real average weekly wages are 5.5 percent lower today than during the Reagan administration. As a result, many families are in debt. Spouses are entering the workforce to help make ends meet, and they raise total family income by about one-third. Yet these same families must pay almost 28 percent of their income to the federal government. In effect, mothers are having to work just to pay off Washington, D.C.

It is useful to put the burden on our families in historical perspective. Washington, D.C., has not always been so greedy. Back in 1954, the last year Republicans were in control of the White House and both houses of Congress, federal taxes amounted to less than the tithe to one's local church—8 percent of total family income. Quite often both parents did not have to work unless they chose to do so. But that's the point: Families were free to choose.

Given the tough going for many middle-class families, our nation must ask: What is to be done? At the very least, we should take note of the ideas that do work. As National Center for Neighborhood Enterprise founder Bob Woodson says, "We must study success." There is no better place to study success than in the states, those laboratories of democracy where ideas can be tested.

Perhaps no state in the 1990s has had more success in solving its economic woes than Michigan. The "old" Michigan of the 1970s and 1980s could have been the poster child of the "Rust Belt." In fact, Michigan unemployment was above the national average for 192 months in a row (1978–1993). By contrast, it has been at or below the national average for the past 28 months. Now, we are being hailed as the center of the nation's "Growth Belt." A *Wall Street Journal* headline summed up the turnaround: "Go West, Young Man!"

Under Republican leadership in the last five years, Michigan has made a dramatic turnaround by:

- eliminating a $1.8 billion deficit;

- balancing the budget five years in a row;

- cutting taxes an incredible 21 times;

- downsizing state bureaucracy while improving services;

- eliminating regulatory red tape.

Michigan is living proof that what the liberal establishment has decreed is impossible is possible. We aren't just talking about "supply-side theory" anymore; we are talking about "supply-side success."

One of our most popular and innovative projects is our newly established Office of Regulatory Reform, which in its first year has cut 1,000 obsolete, burdensome, and often contradictory rules and regulations from the rollbooks of state government. By the time you read this, 1,000 more will be on the chopping block.

Of the 21 tax cuts in our first 60 months in office, the most dramatic was cutting school operating property taxes from an average 36 mills to 6 mills. This was the biggest tax cut in Michigan history, amounting to $3.6 billion. Associated with this cut is a cap that keeps assessments from rising more than the inflation rate. The effect? When I took office in 1991, our property tax burden was the third worst in the nation. Now, our property taxes are below the nation's, and our average millage rate is the lowest it has been in three decades.

We also axed Michigan's erstwhile "intangibles tax" because it was really a capital gains tax and, as such, it had a serious negative impact on savings, dividends, and investment. When we first proposed cutting this tax, liberals went on the attack. Across the state, slanted newspaper, magazine, and television editorials accused Michigan Republicans of trying to help the rich at the expense of the poor and the middle class. They failed to mention that one of their patron saints, President John F. Kennedy, supported tax cuts because, he said, "a rising tide lifts all boats."

But it is reality, not rhetoric, that has proved the liberals wrong. Here is what Michigan's real-life experience has demonstrated: When citizens pay lower taxes on dividend income, they invest more. Their investment pumps more money into the economy and spurs banks to cut interest rates, since there is more cash chasing new projects out there. When the cost of borrowing money is cheaper, manufacturers not only create more jobs and hire more workers but they can buy better equipment, which increases productivity. Greater productivity results in lower costs for consumers and higher wages for workers.

Have Michigan's 21 tax cuts helped or hurt our economy? You be the judge:

- •For three years, Michigan has led the nation in wage increases.

- •For the past two years, our unemployment rate has been consistently lower than the nation's for the first time in a quarter of a century.

- •In 1995, one of every five new manufacturing jobs in America was created in Michigan.

- •Michigan is now widely acknowledged as the high-performance heart of America's heartland.

Ever since the Reagan Revolution, liberal journalists, economists, and politicians have tried to convince Americans that tax cuts are "wacky" and doomed to failure. But in Michigan we have tried them, and we know this: Tax cuts not only work; they work wonders.

Laboratories of Democracy

The states have been called "laboratories of democracy" for good reason. As I indicated earlier, they are the proving grounds for ideas. Compared to the federal government, they are more responsive to the electorate, more efficient when it comes to fulfilling legitimate government functions, more flexible when it comes to trying new approaches, and—let's all cheer—more economical. But for decades now, the states have lost out to an increasingly unresponsive, inefficient, inflexible, and expensive bureaucracy in Washington, D.C. One reason is that this bureaucracy is able to confiscate more and more tax dollars to finance its power grabs.

This confiscation isn't just about the loss of money either. It is about the loss of one of the most precious resources of all: time. Currently, the Internal Revenue Service estimates that Americans spend about 1.7 billion hours on tax-related paperwork by the time their returns are completed. Businesses spend another 3.4 billion hours. As Arizona Senator John Kyl has observed, "If that is not evidence that our tax code is one of the most inefficient and wasteful ever created, I do not know what is."

Restoring money, time, and authority to individual citizens is called "devolution." Its agenda is twofold: First, Congress must balance the budget and reduce taxes. Second, in welfare, Medicaid, job training, and education, Congress must free the states. It must send our revenues back, hold us accountable, and judge us by one criterion—performance.

Welfare Reform

The states will do far better by their citizens than the federal government. How can I be so sure that there won't be a "race to the bottom" once devolution is set in motion? I am sure because I have seen what has already happened in Michigan. "Exhibit A" is our state's extraordinary progress in the area of welfare reform:

- •Because Michigan requires recipients to work, over 89,500 Michigan families have moved from a welfare roll to a payroll.

- •Welfare caseloads are lower in our state than they have been in two decades.

- •In Michigan, almost one in three welfare recipients of Aid to Families with Dependent Children (AFDC) is working; nationally, only one in 12 is working.

- •Abstinence, not "safe sex," has become the focus of our campaign to deter teen pregnancy and single motherhood.

Education Reform

The states are also our best hope for genuine education reform—reform that is desperately needed. Each year, America spends almost $300 billion on education. A student who graduates from a Detroit public school represents an investment of $75,000—that's how much taxpayers spend on his elementary and secondary education. Yet there is good evidence to suggest that many of our graduates are illiterate, and others can only read at a fourth-grade level. It is no wonder that today's businesses are forced to spend an additional $30 billion—in effect, a 10 percent surcharge on what has already been spent—on remedial education for their employees.

Michigan's answer is to improve public schools by introducing market forces that will give families more freedom of choice and inject competition into a monopolistic system. In 1993, the Michigan legislature passed one of the best charter school laws in the nation. In the last three years, more than 40 charter schools have opened their doors. As a result, our state has the third highest number of such schools in the U.S. The demand to enter these schools is proof positive of parents' desire for more choice. The effect is already being felt. One school superintendent told me that the mere possibility of charter schools in his district was encouraging reform throughout the system.

Why is the fight for more school choice and educational quality so important? A recent University of Michigan survey shows that the Big Three will hire as many as 129,000 new workers in our state by the year 2003. They don't need strong backs to do their jobs—they need strong academic skills. Our choice is stark: We either train young people in Michigan today or we lose jobs in Michigan tomorrow. It is that simple. We must do better. We must establish benchmarks for our neighborhood public schools in order to know what the best schools look like and how they get the job done. We must reward excellence and foster competition. And we must make sure our schools measure up to parents' standards and traditional, time-tested values.

Our Moral Patrimony

Above all, we must find ways for all our state governments to help strengthen our moral patrimony. Only if we are a moral people can we be a free and prosperous people. The 18th-century philosopher Adam Smith made this point forcefully in *The Wealth of Nations* and *A Theory of Moral Sentiments*. So, too, have 20th-century writers like economist Ludwig von Mises in *Human Action* and historian Russell Kirk in *The Roots of American Order*.

But the wisdom of the ages reveals that our moral compass cannot ultimately come from Lansing or from any other state capital, any more than it can come from the nation's capital, or Hollywood, or the United Nations, or some abstract liberal conception of the "Village." It comes from deep within us—it comes from our character, which is forged in our families and our faith and tempered in the arena of decisionmaking and action.

LAWRENCE W. REED

Privatization and American Business

With profound disappointment, the great Austrian economist Ludwig von Mises noted that the 20th century will be remembered as an age of statism. At least about that portion of it which he himself observed, Mises was absolutely right.

Statism

Statism—the notion that society's needs and problems are best addressed by politics and the political process—did indeed dominate most of this century's public opinion and public policy. Respect for personal liberties, private property, and freedom of commerce in open, competitive markets fell victim to the state's false but alluring vow of economic security. Governments grew immensely—commanding ever greater portions of personal income, regulating and even nationalizing businesses, making public burdens of millions of people.

Those who supported the free market suffered in number but not in spirit or persistence. Some of the greatest critiques of the interventionist state ever written were penned as the state approached the zenith of its influence. Mises's *Socialism* in the 1920s and Hayek's *The Road to Serfdom* in the 1940s stand as two of the very best examples. For the free market to prevail, however, its friends would sooner or later have to devise a strategy for actually dismantling socialism. Theoretical critiques, though essential to winning the intellectual battle, would have to be supplemented by practical methods of taking what was "public" and making it "private." What had been "socialized" would have to be "privatized."

By the 1970s, the bitter harvest of statism was everywhere apparent: in bloated, overbearing bureaucracies, in crushing tax burdens, and in frightening burdens of debts and deficits. Public officials and private citizens alike began to look for answers. The case for freedom and free markets began to win the battle among intellectuals. Increasing numbers among the general public followed suit, electing public officials committed to stuffing the statist genie back into its bottle. The time for *privatization* had arrived.

Privatization

A definition is in order. Privatization, in its broadest sense, is the transfer of assets or services from the tax-supported and politicized *public* sector to the entrepreneurial initiative and competitive markets of the *private* sector. The superiority of the latter, which Mises once explained as an almost lone voice in the wilderness, is now approaching the status of undisputed, conventional wisdom: The private sector exacts a toll from the inefficient for their poor performance, compels the service provider or asset owner to concern himself with the wishes of customers, and spurs a dynamic, never-ending pursuit of excellence—all without any of the political baggage that haunts the public sector as elements of its very nature.

In an interdependent world getting smaller through the speed of transportation and communications, no community of people can compete successfully without ridding itself of costly public enterprises and liberating the entrepreneurial spirit. Recognition of that fact is at the root of today's dramatic privatization revolution—from Moscow to Manila to my hometown of Midland, Michigan.

Competition, Accountability, and Incentives

The theory is simple but grounded in profound truths about the nature of humans and their response to incentives and disincentives. Tie up the performance of a task with red tape, bureaucracy, and politics within a system that is guaranteed to exist regardless of outcome, and the result is usually mediocrity at great expense. Infuse competition, accountability, and the fear of losing valued customers into the task, and mediocrity becomes the exception, excellence the rule.

Sometimes these lessons must be learned the hard way. Here's an example that proves that point: Before the break-up of the Soviet Union, any foreigner traveling there had to go through state-run tourist bureaus for permission to enter, itineraries, and guides. Since the break-up, many of the 15 former Soviet republics have permitted private tour companies to emerge and some of those companies have even been started by the very bureaucrats who used to work for the state.

In Ukraine several years ago, former state employees formed their own private tour company. One of the first brochures they put together was aimed at convincing English-speaking foreigners to visit—of all places!—Chernobyl, the site of the 1986 nuclear disaster. The brochure proudly announced that the tour included a visit to the concrete sarcophagus that envelops the old reactor, a trip to a nearby radioactive waste dump, and a quick stop at a nearby town populated by radiation-exposed workers whose motto is, "Life is Good . . . But Too Short." The brochure also stated that the tour began and ended with a Geiger counter check. It promised that any tourist needing treatment for radiation exposure would receive it "at no extra charge."

Now, I don't know how this entrepreneurial venture turned out, but my guess is that the company quickly learned a lesson or two about pleasing the customer. Unlike working for a socialized enterprise, merely hanging out a sign or printing up a brochure does not guarantee revenue or a job in a free market. That is a great strength of the free market itself—indeed, it is the main reason why free markets in America have fed, clothed, and housed more people at higher levels than any socialized economy anywhere could even promise.

When it is done properly and with care, privatization harnesses the powerful market forces of competition, accountability, and incentives. It means that government officials don't have to be hemmed in by an indifferent bureaucracy. Instead, they can "shop around," as other consumers do, for the best available buys. State and local governments have routinely experienced cost savings of 10 to 40 percent through privatization and often with accompanying improvements in the way an asset is managed or a service is delivered. When and where assets and services can be left entirely in private hands from the very start, even greater efficiencies are possible.

The most common form of privatization—*contracting out* to private firms—has become more than just a trend. With decades of experience, it has become something of a science at the local level in America. We now know what it takes to make this work: open, competitive bidding for contracts that are subject to periodic renewal; careful writing of the contract terms to incorporate clear language and appropriate safeguards; and effective monitoring of performance to ensure the contract is being carried out as expected, to name a few of the requirements.

Commercialization is another form of privatization. It happens when a unit of government simply says, "We are no longer going to do this work with our own work force. We are not going to contract it out either. We are simply going to get out of this business altogether. The customers we used to serve can take care of the job themselves by contracting with the private provider of their individual choice."

This is how, for instance, cities across America like Traverse City, Michigan, have opted out of the garbage business. The citizens themselves shop amongst several private, competitive firms that specialize in picking up and properly disposing of garbage. No middleman, no taxes, no boring city council meetings to sweat through in order to register a complaint. You hire the service and if you are not happy, you fire it and hire a different one. This form of privatization tends to enhance both our liberties and our pocketbooks if it is done right. Other forms of privatization include:

- the outright gift or sale by government of a physical asset (a piece of equipment or a building, perhaps) to a private entity;

- the issuance of "vouchers" which can be redeemed in the marketplace, instead of direct public provision of a service, giving recipients choices where they had none before;

- the sale of stock in a newly privatized company that was formerly state-owned; and

- the ending of subsidies and all the red tape and regulations that comes with them, liberating an industry to produce "for the market" and not for the government. New Zealand accomplished this with agriculture a decade ago. Farmers there are no longer wards of the state and are prospering in a free market.

A Revolution in Governance

Each of these forms, of course, has its pros and cons. But let there be no mistake about this fact: Privatization in its various forms has now become nothing less than a revolution in governance all over the world. It is happening at a feverish pace, and the more it is done, the more we are learning about how to do it right.

Privatization in Great Britain

Former British Prime Minister Margaret Thatcher taught us much about how to privatize. During her tenure, she sold off seven major commercial airports, including Heathrow, Gatwick, Aberdeen, and Stansted—in a careful, studied, and public way that maximized popular support for the move. More than two million citizens bought 1.4 billion shares of stock in the airport privatization effort.

Moreover, Thatcher sold a million units of public housing by offering them to the tenants at well below market value. The tenants who previously complained about the indifference of distant, bureaucratic management became the owners and managers themselves. With pride of ownership working its wonders, whole neighborhoods were subsequently transformed—broken windows were replaced, broken screen doors were repaired, gardens sprouted where litter once marred the landscape. The British treasury was relieved of the burden of throwing huge subsidies down the rathole of public housing. The experience bears testimony to a time-honored principle of human action: *What you own, you take care of. What nobody or "everybody" owns falls into disrepair.*

Many state-owned companies were privatized under Thatcher—the mammoth British Telecom being the foremost example. To encourage public employees to be supportive, Thatcher offered them first crack at the sale of stock. They could buy the stock at discounts from what shares were expected to fetch later in the open market. The result? Public employees made money and became prideful part owners of new, private firms. The general public enjoyed better services. The British economy became more competitive. And taxpayers saved a bundle of money.

In the space of a decade, Margaret Thatcher sold off $40 billion in state enterprises. The number of British households owning stock rose from 2 million to 12 million. About three-quarters of a million government employees were transferred from public to private payrolls. Once the post-war "sick man of Europe," Britain came to life again.

In a few places around the world, privatization is occurring because the enlightened leaders in power are motivated by ideology. They have *read* the works of Mises, Hayek, Friedman, and other great minds of free market economics. They *know* that free markets work and socialism does not. Prime Minister Vaclav Klaus of the Czech Republic is one such leader, and he has been shedding state assets and services at an impressive pace.

In most places, however, privatization is occurring for more pragmatic reasons. Countries, states, provinces or communities have hit the "tax wall," meaning they have no more room to raise taxes. Doing so would either violate some constitutional or statutory limit, or send people and businesses packing for friendlier climes. In other cases, government simply has not kept pace with technology and productivity advances and must rely upon private enterprise to put its unique expertise to work. So, for pragmatic reasons, hard-pressed politicians are exercising the best or only option they have—they privatize.

Privatization in the U.S.

At the federal level in the United States, little has been privatized but much could be. The power of entrenched bureaucracy and special interests who support the status quo is greater in Washington, as a rule, than it is at the state or local level. Proposals to privatize everything from Social Security to federal lands to the Post Office are now on the table, but they probably await a more friendly White House.

Incidentally, the Post Office is already undergoing a kind of market-driven, *involuntary and unplanned privatization.* Every time you use a private overnight mail service, a fax machine, or electronic computer mail to send a message you might ten years ago have sent via "snail mail," you are personally privatizing the U.S. Postal Service.

At the state level, there's much more going on. States are privatizing utilities, prison management, data processing, foster care, and a long list of other items. Michigan, I am proud to note, set a record in 1994 for the largest sale of an asset (in dollar terms) in the history of all 50 states. The state removed itself entirely from the worker's compensation insurance business when it sold the Accident Fund of Michigan and reaped $255 million in the process.

It is, however, at the local level of government—counties and cities and schools—where the privatization revolution is really taking off. You name it, just about any asset or service that a local government owns or provides has been privatized somewhere, in some manner, partially or wholly. That includes fire protection, certain elements of police protection, waste water treatment, street lighting, tree trimming, snow removal, parking structures, railroads, hospitals, jails, and even cemeteries.

Mayor Steve Goldsmith of Indianapolis is one of the leaders in municipal privatization. According to Reason Foundation experts William Eggers and John O'Leary in their new book, *Revolution at the Roots*, Goldsmith has subjected more than 60 city services to competitive bidding and other forms of privatization. City employees have been given the opportunity to reorganize and enter the bidding too, in competition with private firms, and have won back the right to perform certain services. A funny thing happens when public employees have to directly compete: They discover that they really don't need as many supervisors, make-work rules, and coffee breaks.

Goldsmith has put almost everything Indianapolis does on the list for possible privatization. His motto is enough to make entrepreneurs out of many foot-dragging bureaucrats: "Sacred cows," he says, "make the best burgers." Indianapolis is now one of the best-run cities in the country. It is "lean, mean, and clean," as the saying goes.

But governments don't always have to privatize to get their work done more efficiently. Sometimes, all they have to do is tell the world they're just *thinking* about it. This is the lesson from Flint, Michigan, where Mayor Woodrow Stanley can take credit for saving city residents $1.4 million from an annual $6.2 million garbage collection budget. For months, Mayor

Stanley made it plain to the city that garbage collection was costing too much money. He finally did something about it in early 1994. He solicited bids from five private companies and the numbers confirmed his suspicions. If one of those bids was accepted, the combination of a private firm handling garbage, compost, bulk items, and trash bins and the city taking care of leaf pickup and special clean-ups would cut the city's total cost by a whopping $2 million!

Flint's city employee unions then knew the mayor was serious. They scrambled to be competitive and offered to shave about $1.4 million from the garbage budget. They proposed increasing the number of stops on each route from 665 to 775, reducing the number of shifts from two to one, cutting the sanitation staff from 47 workers to 35, picking up bulk items along with regular garbage instead of doing that on overtime, and requiring workers—get ready for this—to work a full eight-hour day instead of going home early as they often had done in the past! These concessions were sufficient to convince the mayor and city council, at least for the time being, to keep garbage collection in-house and save $1.4 million.

This is just one case where simply going through the motions of privatization was enough to save a small fortune. Mayor Stanley told the *Flint Journal,* "If I were just some weak-kneed kind of namby-pamby politician, I wouldn't have touched this privatization issue with a 10-foot pole. Political leaders who aren't willing to take risks don't deserve to be in office."

Good Stewardship

Considering the privatization option, whether or not the final decision is to actually do it, is nothing less than good stewardship of the public purse. Thinking seriously about it prompts officials to open their minds and think about government services in ways they never pondered before. It forces them to find out, for instance, how much it is actually costing them to provide those services.

Most people don't realize that governments keep their financial books in what can only be described as a state of confusion. Rarely are all the appropriate costs of an activity or department actually charged to it. For example, a county sheriff in Michigan once boasted that he could house prisoners for a mere $17 a day, but a few follow-up questions revealed many things he wasn't counting because "some other department" took care of them—costly items such as custodial work to keep the jail clean and the pension obligations payable to jail employees.

At the Mackinac Center for Public Policy—the nation's premier state-focused, free market think tank—we discovered this important truth when we examined the custodial costs in a half-dozen public school districts around Michigan's capital city of Lansing. None of the districts had ever computed their custodial costs in a fashion that would allow them to gauge just how high they really were. We ran the numbers ourselves and discovered that the least costly district was spending 50 percent more than private firms would charge to do comparable work. The costliest district was spending three to four times more to get the job done! If that single district privatized the work, it would save more than a million dollars a year in custodial bills alone—enough to hire 20 teachers at $50,000 each, or buy 500 computers for $2,500 apiece, or pay for 30,000 textbooks at $33 a book.

The teacher's union, which represents many custodial and food service workers in the schools, didn't appreciate our work. In the face of massive evidence that schools could indeed save money through privatization, the Michigan Education Association actually declared that it would oppose *any* privatization of *any* school support service by *any* school district! Now, you might ask, how can it be demonstrated to the taxpaying public that the MEA's position is purely self-serving and inimical to the interests of the very children the union claims to be educating?

In thinking about this question at the Mackinac Center, it occurred to us that the MEA might not be practicing what it preaches. Surely, we thought, the union does not have its own full-time, fully unionized, in-house work force providing every possible service at its own sprawling headquarters near Lansing. We checked it out and announced our findings in a press release headlined, "Mackinac Center Praises MEA For Cutting Edge Management Techniques."

Sure enough, we discovered that the teacher's union contracts out at its own headquarters with private firms for all of its own food service, custodial work, security, and mailing services and—in three out of four cases—with nonunion firms! The hypocrisy of the union was not lost on the legislature, which eventually granted school districts much greater freedom to privatize support services without having to worry about opposition from the MEA. There is now a budding privatization revolution taking place in Michigan public schools as a result.

Examples of privatization are everywhere. Studies by the dozens verify its effectiveness. Articles and monographs advising officials of the pitfalls to avoid and the strategies that work are proliferating. There is simply no denying that privatization is indeed a major trend now and that each new experience teaches us even more about how to maximize its benefits.

The Truth about Privatization

Objections to it, however, are still heard and sometimes loudly. I share here the most common ones, along with a brief response:

• *It is anti-public employee.* As the experience of innovative cities like Indianapolis proves, strategies can be devised that actually involve public employees in a positive way. But ultimately, we must remember that government does not exist for the benefit of those who work for it; it exists for the benefit of those who pay its bills or need its services. Governments that employ more people than necessary, or that pay their employees more than the market will bear, are not doing any favors for the citizens— including the poor—who are picking up the tab.

- *It is a back-door way to hobble or destroy government.* Mayor Gold-smith says that before he privatized city services, it was extreme-ly difficult to resolve citizen complaints or get the bureaucracy to move on anything. Once a service is privatized, accountability is almost instantaneous. If performance suffers, the city can quickly cancel the contract. Because of that, says the mayor, government officials like him are actually empowered, not hobbled. They can "shop around," just like ordinary consumers, and thereby find the best buys.

- *There are instances where it didn't work, so we shouldn't do it any-where.* I have yet to see a case where a failure was really an indictment of privatization itself. Failures are almost always arguments for avoiding poor practices, such as noncom-petitive bidding in smoke-filled back rooms, sloppy contract writing, or nonexistent monitoring of performance.

- *It can breed special interests.* There are those who fear it will create lobbying for more contracts even when services are unwarranted. But public bureaucracies lobby for more govern-ment, too. This is an argument for taxpayers and the press to be vigilant, not an argument against privatization.

- *Government officials may not do the right thing with the savings.* It's true that when privatization generates lower costs, officials may have multiple options for realizing the gain. They may choose to avoid raising taxes or actually cut them, passing the savings on to taxpayers. Or, they may simply take the sav-ings and squander them on some other dubious enterprise of government. This is, again, an argument for vigilance, not against privatization.

All citizens who value freedom and the free markets that give life to that freedom should be encouraged by the priva-tization revolution. A leaner, better performing public sec-tor is much more than a bipartisan "good government" issue. It is an imperative that when accomplished will leave us a freer, more responsible, and better-served people.

P. J. Meddings

The Global Businessplace and Entrepreneurs

Never before in human history has the ordinary individual, the man in the street, had so many opportunities to choose his way of life. This is an historic time. The men and women who will take advantage of opportunities in the businessplace are the wealth creators—the entrepreneurs who will take our world into a new era of prosperity and progress. This chapter is about these opportunities, as well as the limitations and barriers that still apply, the characteristics of entrepreneurs, and the way any one of us can become one of them. There are many definitions of the word "entrepreneur," and it has a number of connotations. Mine is simple: It refers to those people who start successful enterprises or expand existing ones significantly.

The Opportunities for Entrepreneurs

Where are the opportunities for entrepreneurs? First of all, they exist in the world with which we are familiar—in America, in Europe, in Australia, and elsewhere in the developed world. Hundreds and even thousands of Westerners are starting businesses every day with new or advanced technology or by taking market share from existing businesses. Examples abound of high-tech companies that have started in the last two decades in computing, communication, superconductors, and biomedicine. But traditional businesses offer great opportunities, too. A friend of mine emigrated from South Africa to Australia 15 years ago. He was at a disadvantage because it was a time when it was not possible to transfer money abroad. But he managed to start a business representing an international brand wanting to launch a presence in Australia. He expanded into a number of shops, sold them, and then moved into another altogether different area of retail business. After expanding that enterprise, he sold part of the equity to a world-dominant American corporation and now manages its Australian and Asian operations, with an annual turnover in Australia alone of $300 million. So neither capital nor borders are barrier to entrepreneurs. Neither is age. The most successful entrepreneur of all time, Bill Gates, started with nothing as a teen-ager, dropping out of college to start a then-unknown software company called Microsoft. I started my own business, The Executive Committee, only ten years ago at age 58 after taking early retirement from the corporate world.

But the opportunities for entrepreneurship in the Western world pale in comparison with those emerging in developing countries and the Third World. In recent years, dozens of governments have opened their economies to private enterprise—Russia, the Czech Republic, China, India, Vietnam, Argentina, and Chile are just a few. As a result, the economies of these nations are growing rapidly, particularly in Asia, which is the fastest-growing region in the world. The great free market economist Ludwig von Mises would be delighted by this dramatic extension of economic freedom and prosperity. Some countries in Asia are growing at rates of 6 to 14 percent per annum compared with 3 percent in most Western countries. The standard of living and size of the middle class are also increasing at remarkable rates. The average wage in Singapore and Hong Kong has now surpassed that of Australia, which at the beginning of this century had the one of the highest standards of living in the world.

With this growth, what is the possibility of any of us being involved as entrepreneurs? It is very great, indeed. However, we must remember that the world does not always remain static; some cultures and economies are rising while others are falling. This "cycle of bondage" was described by historian Alexander Tytler (1748-1813) in his book, *The Decline and Fall of the Athenian Republic*. Throughout history, Tytler argued, empires have typically moved:

- from Bondage to Spiritual Faith;

- from Spiritual Faith to Courage;

- from Courage to Liberty;

- from Liberty to Abundance;

- from Abundance to Selfishness;

- from Selfishness to Complacency;

- from Complacency to Apathy;

- from Apathy to Dependency;

- from Dependency to Bondage.

We must ask ourselves, where are we in that cycle in the Western world? I believe that we in the West have, to a large extent, become comfortable, apathetic, and dependent on the largesse of governments. We have forgotten, as Mises taught us, that human behavior is what directs the economy. And where in this cycle are the Asians? Many Asian peoples have recently emerged from bondage and tyranny to enjoy a greater degree of liberty and, to some extent, abundance. *Megatrends* author and futurist John Naisbitt reports that already there are over one million millionaires in China. There is tremendous energy, excitement, and a driving desire to improve in Asia that once existed in our countries and that is now diminished.

However, the opportunities for anyone, including Western-ers, are still considerable if they have the ability, energy and desire to succeed. I have built and run businesses in Malaysia and Indonesia and initiated another in China while I was in the corporate world. My present company, The Executive Com-mittee, involves 3,600 chief executives of companies who meet every month in order to learn how to become more effective. Many of these CEOs are entrepreneurs who have founded and built their own companies in every part of the world. They understand that opportunities often have to be chased down, wherever they exist. I am reminded of the example of one CEO whose Australian construction company took a down-turn; instead of closing shop, he simply expanded into Thailand where his business is now booming.

New Links Around the World

The changes and opportunities for entrepreneurs I have described have arisen in the last two or three decades. But there is another more recent development in the last two or three years that is multiplying their effect many times over. It is the revolution in the electronics and computer indus-tries. Vast databases around the world are now linked and the information in them is available almost instantaneously using Internet. On my portable laptop computer, I have access to a business intelligence program which, within seconds, will allow me to locate almost any information I need from any source. I can access and download information about coun-tries, markets within countries, and companies within mar-kets as quickly and easily as making a local telephone call. And this information can be collected and distilled for me in advance.

I also have e-mail contact with the people in my compa-nies, with member companies associated with us, and with per-sonal contacts around the world. And the technology already exists to be able to see a live picture of the person I am speaking to on my computer screen and to speak with him on Internet. Soon this technology will be within the reach of the average person at a relatively small cost. As with the personal computer, the rate of expansion of technology and its commercial and personal use is limited only by the ability of individuals to learn it.

So how does this revolution impact the opportunities that exist for entrepreneurs around the world? It is obvious, isn't it? We don't have to spend as much time in airplanes, hotels, and taxis. We can make our inquiries and conduct our business personally and instantaneously on our computers and the time and cost involved is greatly reduced. There is no difference between communicating with someone in the next suburb in America and in doing the same with someone in Europe, Australia, or Asia. Of course, some personal contact is necessary to create confidence, carry out negotiations, and so on, but the overall need is greatly reduced.

What Are Our Limitations?

There are no powerful kings to deny us access to their domain, no powerful family merchants to inhibit our entry, no rulers of business to tell us what we can do, no world government. We have arrived at a special moment in time—a window in history—in which every individual has the ability to choose his future. Yet, there are limitations, and, frankly, they are limitations that have tended to stop all but a small percentage of us from becoming entrepreneurs.

Governments

Governments are the institutions that impose the most limitations. They often unwittingly discourage honest creativity and encourage dishonest creativity. They do so by destroying the will of many individuals with welfare and by overtaxing and overregulating others. Overregulation is particularly trou-

blesome for would-be entrepreneurs and new start-up businesses. An Australian businessman recently reported, for example, that he had to apply for 84 approvals in order to start
a new subsidiary in the mining business. Governments also
erect barriers to trade and overseas investment. And, in all
their actions, they seem to have little or no regard as to how
they affect human behavior in the marketplace.

But they cannot stop the real entrepreneur. Except in the worst
dictatorships, entrepreneurs the world over are embracing private enterprise and flourishing, no matter what the restrictions placed on them. Entrepreneurs will always out-think the
government. They will even start businesses to tell other
entrepreneurs how to outwit government! Governments may
change the goal posts, but they cannot change the game, because the game is human endeavor and achievement.

In fact, the restrictions placed by governments can be used
to the entrepreneur's advantage. In starting the Malaysian factory that I mentioned earlier, the government supported the
proposal, which increased employment and introduced an industry which otherwise would not exist, by placing a tariff
barrier on imported, competitive products (a move Mises and
other free market advocates would not support) and giving
us an eight-year, tax-free holiday (a move that they would not
only support but encourage). And if, on occasion, a government stops entrepreneurs in one country, they can move to
another—or they can simply move their capital, which several modern economists have likened to "quicksilver," since
it has become so mobile.

Funding

But finding the initial funds to start a business is often a
problem for entrepreneurs, particularly for younger men and
women who have not had the opportunity to build up capital. In the past, their source of funds has usually been found
in their local community—through family, friends, banks,

and venture capitalists. However, with the advent of fast communication and readily available information, this source has been expanded to take in the world community. There is no shortage of cash in the world. What lenders are looking for are the right people and the right project—in that order. My advice to younger entrepreneurs would be to start a small business that requires little capital and build it up or to develop an excellent, credible business plan and negotiate good terms.

Culture

It is often said that America and the United Kingdom are two countries separated by a common language. I would have thought that Australia and the United Kingdom were very close culturally, but when I moved from Australia to England to start up my business there, I found that there were many minor differences that eventually required major alterations in strategy. It was then I was reminded that the greatest threat to future success is present success. A successful business in Australia does not guarantee that the same business will be successful elsewhere, even in the United Kingdom. It is a lesson that I always remember.

How different are the cultures of the West and the East? The answer is "very different," and the differences must be taken into account by any entrepreneur. In Chinese society, for example, the fundamental model is the extended family. Very often, the success of a negotiation is not dependent on how you portray yourself to the negotiator but on whether his father, who is lurking in the back room, likes you and your proposal. And something that is quite acceptable to a person in one province of China might be an insult to someone in another province. These are not impassable roadblocks, but they do need to be understood before they are overcome. Because of the extended family and the necessity to protect the family name, much business in China is done through mutual contacts. So, developing such contacts and establishing trust is a first step to doing business in the East.

Capability

Entrepreneurs take risks, or so it is said. My own belief is they take no more risks than anyone else for the simple reason that to not take a risk is itself a risk. It is a risk of dullness, a risk of living at the behest of others and being dependent on them for the quality of your life. What is important is the sort of risk that one takes. Unfortunately, too many entrepreneurs take poor risks, and they have a high failure rate. About 60 percent of all small firms don't survive beyond their fifth year, mainly because of poor management, particularly poor financial management.

The fact is that many entrepreneurs start businesses without any previous experience or training, and many fail as a result. To avail oneself of the opportunities that exist in the world, it is essential to have had some experience or training or both, unless one uses mentors and advisors very well and constantly. Nobel laureate Friedrich A. Hayek developed this cardinal principle: No one individual can know it all. How right he was! My advice to new entrepreneurs is to learn some aspects of management well; to be able to read and interpret balance sheets and income statements and to prepare budgets; to know something about marketing strategy and selecting and handling people. Then, they should join a company and gain experience. It doesn't matter whether it has good or bad management, because they may learn from both.

Willingness and Desire

None of the above limitations, together or singly, are sufficient to stop the determined entrepreneur. Governments create hurdles that can be jumped. Funding can be found for the right person and project. Culture can be discovered. Capabil-

ity can be learned. The only real barrier to entrepreneurship is the willingness and desire of the individual to partic-
ipate and succeed.

The only valid reason for not becoming an entrepreneur
is choosing not to. It is perfectly valid to choose the corporate life, the academic life, the political life, or some other
kind of life, but we must be clear that we are making a choice
of our own accord, not because of external limitations, because
these, no matter what they are, can be conquered.

The Way We Are

In my company, we recently conducted a survey of 80 chief
executives of small- to medium-sized companies with turn-
overs of $4 million to $100 million. The first question was:
"Which is most important in being a successful chief executive—information, knowledge, experience, or the way we
are?" Every one of the 80 respondents said that the way we
are is the most important. Yet think for a moment. Do we select
people on the way they are, or on the basis of their resume?
In my experience, the resume means very little, but we depend on it too much. The following personal attributes are
some of those that were identified by the respondents to be
the most important ones necessary to be a successful CEO.
I endorse them and believe that they are also necessary to
become a successful entrepreneur.

Passion and Vision

The first requirement of an entrepreneur is that he must
have a strong driving force or passion—security, money, the
approval of others, a drive to excel, a desire to be independent, or the need to fulfill a vision. Although the first three
can be powerful, they are not enough in the long-run; they
either fade or result in failure. So, to be successful, the last

three are more important. In my case, the forces that drive me are a need to contribute back to business what I have gained from it, a vision of how to do that, and a passion for the process that I have chosen to share my talents and experience.

Brightness and Energy

I know what I mean by brightness, and yet I have the greatest difficulty defining it. It is not intelligence, because some highly intelligent people can be narrow and dull. It is not empty-headed extroversion. It is not a happy smile necessarily. It has something to do with alertness, empathy, curiosity in all things, the ability to understand situations, to make decisions that are sensible, open-mindedness, and encouraging others with one's leadership. It has little to do with education, although bright people usually seek to be educated.

I have a friend whose family, like mine, was working class. In order to make some pocket money while he was in school, he cut pencils in half and sold the halves at an exorbitant price to the racing punters in the local pub who never had a pencil available. He had street wisdom at an early age, and he has had it ever since. He also has a keen interest in and understanding of other people. He now runs one of Australia's largest companies. He is bright.

By contrast, watching TV a few weeks ago gave me an excellent example of the deadening effect of welfare. A young man was interviewed who had been on the dole and now was halfway through a computer course the government was paying him to take. The subsidy had just been repealed, and the reaction of the young man was that he could no longer learn computing and would just have to rely on the dole. He felt this way despite the fact that local councils have free facilities and courses in most suburbs. Where is the brightness here?

Allied to brightness is energy. Nothing happens in business unless someone makes or sells something. All the planning in the world is useless unless someone does something.

And the doing requires energy. Brightness and energy go hand in hand.

Courage

In my experience, which is borne out by the experience of many other entrepreneurs, for every person who supports a new venture, there will be ten who tell you, seriously and authoritatively, that it can't be done. I have many friends in southern California. Often when I see them, one of them will ask: "Where are you going to start up next? I wish I had the opportunity to start a business in another country." My reply is always: "You do. Mexico is only 30 miles away." But they never do.

Courage is more than bravery. Courage is knowing what you are doing, being aware of the risks, and still doing it. It is being willing to confront people in authority. It is being willing to move anywhere, to work night and day if necessary, to make little money for a start, to work from the second bedroom, to make decisions with the best knowledge available, and to follow them with actions. Without courage, you will never be an entrepreneur.

Persistence

Sometimes an entrepreneurial venture works immediately. Then you are lucky. Very often unforeseen barriers appear that deter many people. Setbacks will occur. Mistakes will be made. We all make them. Persistence and resilience are characteristics that I see with the associates of The Executive Committee. I sit with them in many meetings discussing key business issues. Even I shake my head in amazement at their willingness to persist when faced by what seems an insurmountable problem. And yet they are flexible as well, maintaining their major goals but changing as circumstances change.

Values and Integrity

Crooks don't win in the long run. The history of the 1980s in most Western countries is recent proof. Using shareholders' and investors' money for personal gain, to the detriment of the company, is usually found out and punished accordingly. Even apparently small things like delaying the payment of bills, which is thieving, or being consistently late for appointments, which is not keeping agreements, is evidence of some lack of integrity. These things sound minor because they have often been accepted in our world. But they are not minor in many other parts of the world where they can indicate untrustworthiness and they can cause projects to be lost and ventures to fail.

So there are good business reasons to maintain values and have integrity. But business is only part of life, isn't it? Is participation in shady deals, negotiating so that others lose, destroying the environment, exploiting the ignorant, evading taxes and generally, if not breaking the law, living on that fine edge, the way we want to live our lives? I doubt it. We want our world to become a better place, and for that we must know and define our values and maintain them with integrity.

How Do I Want to Be?

I am mindful that young people are the ones who will determine the future of business. They often ask themselves, "What do I want to do?" People always want to know what to do, but the far more important question is, "How do I want to be?" And so the wise statement of Lord Polonius is just as applicable to budding entrepreneurs as it was to Laertes: "This above all, to thine ownself be true...."

In 1902, George Lorimer wrote a wonderful book titled, *Letters from a Self-Made Merchant to His Son.* If I were writing to my young son today, what would I say to do? I believe my advice would be something like this:

At school and at college, learn to learn in such a way that you never lose your desire and you continue to learn for the rest of your life. Read about other cultures and visit some if you can. Learn several languages. Be familiar with computers and communications and maintain the state of that art. Establish your values and know them well. But be open-minded and ready to change with new information. Become very good at something. Make contacts and trusting friends, particularly with students and others from overseas and realize that the world is not just what lies at your doorstep but what lies beyond. Cut pencils and dream.

After school, if you wish to be an entrepreneur, go off-shore and experience the world. Learn from people in other countries. Make more contacts and gather a small circle of mentors and advisors. Keep in touch personally and on Internet. Know yourself and your capabilities. Then take your courage in both hands and do it. The world is your oyster. The opportunities are immense, and the only barrier is ourselves.

LUDWIG VON MISES

Small and Big Business

A characteristic feature of the contemporary policies of all the not outright socialist nations is animosity against business. Public opinion contrasts the mean selfishness of those engaged in the conduct of business with the lofty altruism of the politicians and the public servants. The profits made by those enterprises that succeed in filling, in the best possible and cheapest way, the most urgent wants of the consumers, i.e., of everybody, are called "unearned" income in the tax laws and are subject to confiscatory and discriminatory imposts. To restrict as much as possible the sphere in which private enterprise is free to operate—the so-called private sector of a nation's economy—and to expand concomitantly the public sector is considered as one of the foremost goals of economic policies. While paying lip service to the principle of free enterprise, nations are step by step adopting the principles of socialism and totalitarianism.

In spite of all the obstacles put in its way, private enterprise demonstrates anew each day its incomparable efficiency. New and better products appear again and again on the market

Paper presented at the 1961 (Turin, Italy) meeting of the Mont Pelerin Society. Reprinted with permission from Bettina Greaves, ed., *Economic Freedom and Interventionism: An Anthology of Articles and Essays by Ludwig von Mises* (Irvington-on-Hudson, NY: Foundation for Economic Education, 1990).

and are made accessible to the many, not only to a small minority of privileged nabobs. The "common man" enjoys in the capitalistic countries amenities of which the richest people of ages gone by did not even dream. Not so long ago the socialist critics of capitalism used to blame the market economy for the penury of a part of the population, that is, for the fact that capitalism had not yet totally wiped out the unfortunate effects of the precapitalistic methods of production. Today they criticize capitalism for the "affluence" of the private citizen and suggest methods for depriving them of a great part of this "affluence" in order to enable their rulers to spend more for objectives for which the individual citizens do not spend, obviously because they do not approve of them.

The only goal of production is to provide for consumption in the best possible and cheapest way. To serve the consumers is the objective of all business activities. Profits can be earned only by supplying the consumers in the best possible and cheapest way with all those things they want to use. In the market economy the consumers—the people—are supreme.

In competing for the patronage of the consumers, the capitalistic factory outstripped the traditional handicrafts that had prevailed in precapitalistic ages. Romantic dreamers whose information about the old artisans stems from works such as Richard Wagner's *Meistersinger[1]* may deplore this fact. But consumers are now getting more, better, and cheaper shoes than in the time of artisan cobblers. It would be a boon for the barefooted masses of India if the old-fashioned workshops of their shoemakers had to give way to modern shoe factories.

Small Businesses

In the present there is in capitalistic countries, by and large, no longer a keen rivalry between big business and small business. There are lines in which the small-size enterprise can hold its own. Again and again changes in technological conditions and in marketing methods give bigger enterprises the opportunity to enter fields which hitherto have been a domain of small outfits. But on the other hand new specialties develop in which the small shop prevails. There is still room left for small-scale enterprise not only in the repair business, in the service trades, and in some fields of retailing, but even in some highly specialized processing jobs and certainly also in many categories of agriculture.

It is, of course, misleading to seek from statistics information about the role small units play in the structure of modern business. The features on the basis at which statistics classify an outfit as independent refer to legal, administrative, and technological characteristics. They qualify as independent businesses many jobs that substantially depend on a big-size concern. In many branches the distribution of the products and the rendering of the various services which the buyer expects and regularly gets from the seller is customarily accomplished by firms or individuals whose business has the legal character of an autonomous existence, although it is essentially merely an outlet of a big concern.

Neither can we obtain more reliable information about the actual number of flourishing small business outfits by observing the purchasing habits of people. Even in the shopping districts of the big urban agglomerations we see interspersed among the numerous outlets of chain stores a rather impressive variety of seemingly independent retailers and artisans. But here again it is impossible, without a searching scrutiny of every individual case, to sift those that are really independent from those that are not.

A substantial antagonism between big concerns and small independent businessmen still prevails in retailing. Chain stores, department stores, and supermarkets are annexing more and more of the field previously served by the small shopkeeper. In almost every country trade associations of small businesses try to delay or even to stop this evolution. They aim at a privileged position for themselves and at legal and

administrative restriction of the operations of their financially more potent competitors. Public opinion sympathizes
with their claims and political parties promise to support them.
But the consumers do not back up these endeavors. More and
more people stop patronizing the small shops and turn to their
competitors.

Those trade associations and pressure groups of small businesses that plan to improve the competitive power of their members' outfits by legislative measures, restricting the operations
of big-scale enterprises, are engaged in a hopeless venture.
In the long run the consumers will not acquiesce in a policy
the costs of which would burden them heavily.

Measures to "Help" Small Businesses

The main argument advanced in favor of measures aiding the
small independent shop in its competition with bigger enterprises refers to the moral and civic values inherent in economic independence. People contrast the position of a businessman
who is his own boss and is responsible only to himself with
that of an employee who is integrated in a huge apparatus and
subject to a hierarchy of superior officers. Whatever weight
this argument may have, it is out of place in justifying government intervention for the benefit of definite groups of businessmen. The more effective the government's measures of
such intervention become, the more do they deprive its ben-
eficiaries of their autonomy and their independence. The outward appearance of economic independence may be retained,
but in fact the beneficiary of government support turns more
and more into a ward of the administration. He is no longer
a self-reliant citizen, but depends on the disposition of government officers and politicians. His discretion is restricted
and finally entirely nullified by a bureaucratic apparatus. The
policy inaugurated for the preservation of independent middle class individuals leads to subjecting them to a virtual
guardianship.

The best example is provided by the American farm policy. Its objective was to preserve the "family farm" and the free independent farmer, the type of man that made the United States and laid the foundations of its greatness. But the champions of farm aid were not aware of the insoluble contradiction between the ideal aimed at and the methods resorted to for its realization. A farmer supported by the government at the expense of the rest of the population, the immense majority of the people, is no longer independent. The government tells him what to produce and in what quantity, and thus virtually converts him into a public servant. The free farmer depended on the market; his income came from the consumers. The supported farmer depends on the discretion of a huge apparatus of government agencies. He is the lowest subordinate of a hierarchy of superiors. It is true that at the top of this hierarchy stand the President and Congress in whose election he cooperates. Because they canvass his votes, the politicians promise him aid. But it is precisely this aid that necessarily obliterates his independence. One cannot subsidize a man to render him independent. The very fact of receiving aid deprives the recipient of his discretion to determine the conduct of his affairs. This is the dilemma that the men who, in the last years, directed the course of American farm policies had to face, and could not solve because it cannot be solved.

It is the same in all other spheres of business. If the government grants privileges to certain categories of small business, it must neatly circumscribe the conditions that entitle a man to claim these privileges and must enforce these regulations. But then the privileged entrepreneur forfeits his independence and turns into a subordinate of the administrative apparatus entrusted with the enforcement of the law.

There is need to stress the fact that the terms "small business" and "big business" are rather vague and that the classification of a unit of a business as big or small is different in different countries and has changed considerably with the passing of time. Those politicians and reformers who in the last decades of the 19th century in some of the continental countries of Europe aimed at legislation measures to protect "small business" against the competition of bigger enterprises, were guided by a nostalgic desire to re-establish the conditions of the precapitalistic ages in which artisans—such as tailors, shoemakers, carpenters, and bakers—prevailed in many or most of the branches of processing. But the ideas that inspired in the eighties of the past century the German Baron Vogelsang and the Austrian Prince Liechtenstein find today hardly any support. Perhaps they are a factor in the popular appeal of the French Poujade movement.[2] But no nation can today seriously consider "abolishing" factories and chain stores and replacing them with independent artisans or with cooperative organizations of craftsmen. In the field of the processing industries the era of the handicrafts is gone.

In the industrially most advanced countries people in speaking nowadays of small business in production more often than not have in mind enterprises that in regard to the amount of capital invested, the size of their turnover, and the number of employees, fifty or a hundred years ago would have been called big business. These companies and firms are called small only when compared with the mammoth concerns. Here again we must realize that statistics do not provide any reliable information about the number of such really independent enterprises. For many of the corporations belonging to this group are more or less controlled or even fully owned by big concerns.

In dealing with these medium-size business units one must stress the fact that what makes it rather inconvenient for such enterprises to preserve their independence and causes them to sell out to bigger concerns is very often conditions that are not the effect of the state of the market, but of government policies. While the governments and political parties pretend to condemn "concentration," they are committed to policies that are furthering it.

A typical example: An enterprising man in his twenties starts a new business. He succeeds very well and after twenty or thirty years of strenuous work his firm is rather flourishing. But then it is time for the owner to think of what may happen after his death. His heirs will be liable to pay inheritance taxes of a height that will force them to sell the outfit. Such forced sales bring much less than the price that corresponds to the real worth and net yield of the going business. It could happen that the family will retain but little after having paid their tax liability. In view of these possibilities it appears to the owner more advantageous to sell, while he is still in full vigor, to a big concern for a price paid in stock of the buying corporation. These securities have a broad market and his heirs will be able to sell them without any discount. The inheritance tax will deprive them of a part of the heritage, but not of more than the law was designed to impose upon them.

Capitalism Is Mass Production

Capitalism is mass production for the provision of the masses. The many, the same people who are working in the offices, the shops, the factories, and the farms, consume the greatest part of all the products turned out. In their capacity as consumers they make small enterprises grow into big businesses and force inefficient enterprises to go out of business. It is the efficiency of business, especially also of the biggest—the mammoth—concerns, that provides the masses with the comparatively high standard of living that the common man, the "proletarian" of the Marxian terminology, enjoys in the capitalistic countries. Any further improvements in the average standard of living can be expected only from a still further development of bigness in business. Governmental measures designed to curb big business are slowing down or entirely checking further progress in the material well-being of the masses. They prejudice the interests of the consumers. The bigger an industrial or commercial concern is, the more it depends on the patronage of the masses and the more it is eager to satisfy them.

In the precapitalistic past there was a broad gulf between the voluptuous habits of the well-to-do and the strained circumstances of the many. There was a sharp distinction between the luxuries of the rich and the necessities of the poor. From its very beginnings business, by improving the methods of production, was intent upon making accessible to a greater number of people many of the amenities previously enjoyed only by a tiny minority of wealthy people. But it still took a long time, sometimes many centuries, until an innovation lost its character as a luxury of the few and turned into a commonly used necessity. Capitalism has more and more shortened this period of transition and finally succeeded in virtually eliminating it. In the case of the motor car it still took several decades before the new vehicle turned from a pastime of playboys into an implement of every family. But with the new products developed by contemporary big business this time lag is so short that it practically does not count any longer. There was no sensible period in which the canned and frozen foods, the new textile fibers, radio and television sets, moving pictures, and many other innovations were only within the reach of the wealthy. Products of big business as they are, they can only be designed for mass consumption.

In the precapitalistic ages the difference between rich and poor was the difference between traveling in a coach and four and traveling, sometimes without shoes, on foot. Today in the industrialized parts of the U.S. the difference between rich and poor is the difference between a late model Cadillac and a secondhand Chevrolet. It is difficult to see how this result could have been achieved without bigness in business.

The instigators of the campaign against bigness in business know very well that there cannot be any question of splitting up the large concerns into medium-size enterprises and of preventing the further growth of firms into bigness. They expatiate about the alleged evils of big business in order to make popular their socialist program. They aim at "social control of business," i.e., at subjecting the conduct of business to the control of government agencies.

Nationalization

The original socialist, or communist, scheme as advanced by the pre-Marxian socialists, the Marxians, the Prussian "state socialists," and the Russian Bolshevists, aimed at wresting the conduct of business from private citizens and transferring it to the government. In order to distinguish his own brand of socialism from that of his foremost rival, the German socialist, Ferdinand Lassalle (1825-1864), Karl Marx substituted the term "society" (*Gesellschaft*) for the terms "state" and "government." And he substituted the term "socialization" (*Vergesellschaftung*) of the means of production to distinguish his doctrine from "nationalization" (*Verstaatlichung*), as practiced by the German Chancellor Prince Otto von Bismarck (1815-1898). But the term "socialization" as employed by the German Social-Democrats and the Second International did not mean anything other than "nationalization." The distinction between "socialization" and "nationalization" was merely verbal, a makeshift invented to cope with the special conditions of the German political scene in the age of Bismarck and his successors in office. Both terms signified the same, viz., to take over plants hitherto operated by private citizens and to manage them by government employees. In this sense Lenin approved the opinion that the post office is "an example of the socialist system." He declared as the aim of socialism "to organize the *whole* national economy like the postal system" and promised that "this will free the laboring classes."[3]

What Marx, Lenin, and all their followers failed to see was the fact that all-round nationalization was impracticable in a modern industrial economy. The very idea of nationalization had been hatched by people who lacked the mental capacity to grasp the essential characteristics of the market economy. They looked upon the existing structure of business as upon something permanent. They planned to expropriate the various plants and shops and then to operate them in the way the expropriated "exploiters" had done. They failed to realize the fact that what matters is to adjust daily anew the conduct of affairs to changing conditions and that the eminence of the entrepreneurial system is in its unceasing craving after improvement and the satisfaction of previously latent needs. The entrepreneurs are not people who simply continue what has already been accomplished before. They are essentially innovators, creators of things never heard of previously. This is what those have in mind who speak of the "dynamism" inherent in the capitalistic system of production.

When a nation turns to all-round nationalization of industry, it deprives its people of the benefits they derived from this capitalistic "dynamism." The fanatically anti-capitalistic mentality of our age made the masses in Russia acquiesce in this outcome. It is probable that also the German people would have submitted to these effects willy-nilly if the Germans had adopted Bolshevist methods after their defeat in the first World War. However, the economic conditions of Germany made it impossible to proceed in this way.

Post-World War I Germany

Germany—like most of the other countries of Central and Western Europe—is a predominantly industrial country. This means it cannot feed and clothe its population and supply it with the most urgently needed manufactures out of domestic resources. It must import foodstuffs and many badly needed raw materials. It has to pay for these imports by exporting manufactures, most of them produced out of imported raw materials. It must compete on foreign markets with the industries of all other industrial nations. If its exports drop considerably, starvation must result. In 1918 all German political parties were ideologically biased against private enterprise and in favor of nationalization. But the experience of several decades of nationalized and municipalized enterprises had shown them the inefficiency of public conduct of economic affairs. They were clear-sighted enough to realize that concerns operated by bureaucrats, according to the pattern of the postal service, would not be able to rebuild the German export trade shattered by the events of the four years of war. Not only the "bourgeois," but no less the majority of those who voted the Social-Democratic ticket were fully aware of the fact that only the much-abused "exploiters" and "jobbers" could succeed in competing in foreign markets with the businessmen of all other nations. For Germany in 1918 there could not be any question of imitating the Soviet policies. The hard facts of Germany's economic situation caused Karl Kautsky [German socialist, 1854-1938] and his party comrades who, for many decades had impetuously advocated full socialization, to shrink from the realization of their program. Of course, they were not keen enough to see that their resignation implied the abandonment of the essential policies recommended by the first [fl. 1864-1874] and the second [fl. 1889-1914] Socialist International, and were bitterly offended when Lenin branded them as "social traitors."

The attitude that the German "majority socialists" adopted in 1918 and 1919 marks a turning point in the socialist movement in the countries of Western industrial civilization. The nationalization issue receded more and more into the background. Only some adamant visionaries, entirely blinded by Marxian dogmatism and unfit to face reality, still cling in Germany, England, and the United States to the outworn nationalization slogan. With all other foes of the market economy the party cry is now "planning."

While the nationalization scheme was, at least in principle, developed by British and French authors, the all-round planning scheme is of German origin. In the first World War the

German government, adopting the socialist ideas of Walter
Rathenau (1867-1922), "centralized" one branch of business
after the other, i.e., deprived the individual firms and corporations of the power to direct the conduct of their business affairs. Control of their enterprises was transferred to
a committee whose members—the nominal entrepreneurs of
the branch concerned—were merely an advisory board of a
commissary appointed by the Reich's government and bound
to obey its orders. Thus the government obtained virtual
control of those branches of business that were most important for the provision of the armed forces. As the war went
on, the authorities proclaimed in the "Hindenburg plan" the
application of this system for all branches of German trade
and production. But the Hindenburg program was not yet completely put into effect when the Kaiser's Reich collapsed and
its administrative apparatus disintegrated.

As long as the war lasted, people grumbled about this system called "war socialism" or "Zwangswirtschaft" (compulsory
economy). However, it became popular as soon as it had been
abolished. In spring of 1919 a memorandum drawn up by Rudolf
Wissell and Richard G. O. von Moellendorff proclaimed planning (*Zwangswirtschaft*) as the royal road toward socialism and
the only program proper for a sincerely socialist party. Hence-
forth the parties dubbed as the "right" openly advocated it,
while the parties of the "left" undecidedly wavered between
the support of planning (*Zwangswirtschaft*) and that of nationalization. When in 1930 Heinrich Bruning, an outstanding member of the Catholic Centrum Party, was appointed
Chancellor, he began to prepare the return to all-round planning
that a short time later was consummated by Hitler. The innovations added to the *Zwangswirtschaft* scheme by Hitler were
merely verbal, such as the substitution of the term *Betrieb-
sfuhrer* (shop manager) for the term entrepreneur, the revival of the feudal term *Gefolgschaft* (retinue) to signify a plant's
total labor force, and the suppression of the term "labor market."

Socialism in the United States and Great Britain

In the United States, the National Industrial Recovery Act (NIRA) of 1933 was an attempt to impose at one stroke the *Zwangswirtschaft*. The attempt failed because the Supreme Court declared the act unconstitutional. But as planning remained the great slogan of American leftism, entrepreneurial discretion in the conduct of business has been step by step restricted by vaguely defined powers delegated to an array of administrative agencies.

Great Britain in the second World War adopted by and large the war socialism of the German pattern. But the Labour Party in its stubborn dogmatism failed to realize the fact that this system of central planning was the only form of socialism that could be considered in a predominantly industrial country dependent on the export of manufactures. Just as the German Marxians had done during the first World War, they rejected war socialism as a "bourgeois" makeshift to which the appellation socialism ought to be denied. They proclaimed nationalization as the only method of converting a market economy into a socialist regime. They nationalized the Bank of England, the railroads, the coal mines, and the steel industry. However, this belated revival of the nationalization issue did not substantially affect the trend of British pro-socialist policies. As in the United States, Germany, and the other predominantly industrial countries, in Great Britain too the pro-socialist tendencies manifest themselves today [1961] chiefly in the advocacy of planning, i.e., of measures restricting the individual enterprises' discretion by subjecting them more and more to "social control," i.e., to the control of government agencies.

"Social Control" or "Planning"

The characteristic feature of this system of social control or planning is to be seen in the fact that it preserves to some extent a sphere in which the initiative of the entrepreneurial spirit can benefit the consumers. The heads of the industrial and commercial concerns are still free to devise improvements and measures to adjust the operation of their plants to the changing conditions of the market. Of course, their discretion is limited by the powers assigned to the bureaucrats. But the inefficiency, indolence, and laxity of some of these controllers prevents them from crippling altogether the initiative of business. A modicum of initiative is still left to the enterprising promoter, especially in matters of foreign trade.

The greatest of all the achievements of capitalism is to be seen in the fact that in spite of all the obstacles put in its way by governments and by labor unions it still continues to supply the masses with more, better, and cheaper goods. While governments, political parties, bureaucrats, and union bosses are indefatigably intent upon sabotaging the operations of business, private enterprise still succeeds in improving the services it renders to consumers. We can only guess what these much-maligned speculators, promoters, and jobbers could do for the benefit of the people if their initiative were not enchained by the policies of the welfare state.

The reasons why the powers that are prefer, although reluctantly, the "social control" or "planning" system to the system of nationalization are, not to be seen in the inestimable bounties that accrue to the consumers. Politicians care little about such things. What counts for them is, apart from the considerations of export trade, the effect of the two systems upon government finance.

Take the case of the American railroads. The railroad companies are subject to the most rigid control on the part of various government agencies. The government determines the height of the rates the companies are permitted to charge for the services they render to travelers and to shippers. The government agencies cooperate with the unions in fixing the height of the wage rates the employees receive. They connive at the system of featherbedding which forces the companies to support a host of idle loafers. They force the companies to run trains for which the demand of the public is so small that their operation involves substantial losses. They prohibit many reforms that would reduce waste and unnecessary expenditure; they are especially opposed to mergers. Besides, the companies are hurt by heavy discriminatory taxation on the part of the local authorities. Yet most of the companies have avoided bankruptcy and earn surpluses out of which they have to pay to the federal government millions in taxes.

Now compare this with the conditions of nationalized railroad systems operating in other countries. The management of most of these nationalized railroads involves year after year of considerable losses, and their deficits must be made good by contributions out of the government's revenue from taxes. For the United States Treasury the railroads—and equally the telegraph and the telephone systems—are a source of revenue. For many countries the nationalized railroads and telegraph and telephone systems are an item of expenditure. If the American postal system were operated by private enterprise, it would, even when subject to the control of some government agencies, probably not only render better and cheaper service to the public but also produce a surplus of revenue over costs. It would figure in the federal budget, not as an item of great expenditure, but as a source of revenue. Whatever one may think about the inherent faults of the system of "social control" of business or "planning," the fact remains that it is, at least in its present shape, in every regard superior to nationalization, the alternative system of socialist management.

Government Regulation

The antagonism between the two methods available for the transformation of the capitalistic market economy into a socialist system dominates present-day economic discussion. There is practically no longer any political party that would stand for the unhampered market economy. What the politicians nowadays call economic freedom is a system in which the government "regulates" the conduct of business by innumerable decrees and administrative orders and prohibitions. The Western nations do not endorse the Soviet methods of all-round nationalization of all enterprises and farms. But they no less reject the market economy which they smear as Manchesterism [the theory of 19th-century advocates of free markets], laissez-faire system, or economic royalism. They give to their own system various names such as New Deal, Fair Deal, or New Frontier in the United States, and "*soziale Marktwirtschaft*" in Germany. The authorities credit their own activities that in manifold ways paralyze the entrepreneurial initiative to introduce improvements in the methods of production and to improve the people's standard of living, and they blame business for all the mischiefs resulting fromtheir own interference with it.

Not only the politicians and bureaucrats committed to these policies of progressively restricting the sphere of private business, but also the authors of books and essays dealing with these problems fail to realize that their program leads no less to integral socialism than to the nationalization program. If it is within the jurisdiction of the authorities to determine which prices, wage rates, interest rates, and profits are to be considered as fair and legal and which are not, and if the police and the penal courts are called upon to enforce these decisions, the essential functions of business are transferred to the government. There is no longer any market and no longer a market economy. It is obvious that the countries this side of the Iron Curtain are more and more approaching this state of affairs. The businessmen, threatened by the menace of such controls, are well aware of the fact that they can escape the enactment of "controls," i.e., full government control of all prices, only if they avoid asking prices of which public opinion does not approve. They have long since virtually lost any influence upon the determination of wage rates. Moreover there cannot prevail any doubt about the fact that the bulk of the funds required for financing the ambitious plans for additional government projects will be collected by taxing away what is still left of the "unearned income" of the shareholders. Even with the present height of the rates of income and inheritance taxation, the greater part of the capital invested in business will in a few decades be expropriated and government-owned.

What the advocates of planning and of social control of business consider as a fair arrangement of economic conditions is a state of affairs in which the various enterprises do precisely what the authorities want them to do and every individual's income after taxes is determined by the government. Although all political parties again and again protest their abhorrence of the Hitler regime, they are eager to duplicate Hitler's economic methods. This is what they have in mind when talking about "discipline." They do not realize that discipline and control are incompatible with freedom. Obsessed with the idea that the entrepreneurs and capitalists are irresponsible autocrats and profits are an unfair lucre, they want to deprive the consumers of the power to determine, by their buying and abstention from buying, the course of all production activities, and to entrust this power to the government.

The political corollary of the supremacy of the consumers in the market economy is the supremacy of the voters under the system of representative government. Where the individuals *qua* consumers become wards of the government, representative government gives way to the despotism of a dictator.

Bureaucratic Management

Among the many spurious arguments advanced against big business, the reproach of bureaucratization plays an important but somewhat peculiar role. Those censuring big business for bureaucratization implicitly admit that the business method of profit management is by far superior to bureaucratic management. But, they maintain, with the growth into bigness an enterprise necessarily becomes more and more bureaucratic. The subjection of an economic system in which big concerns prevail, to the supremacy of a governmental bureaucracy, therefore does not amount, they say, to a substitution of the less efficient bureaucratic methods of management for the more efficient profit management. It merely means the replacement of one bureaucracy by another bureaucracy. It will therefore not result in a diminution of the quantity and an impairment of the quality of the goods available for consumption. It is certainly true that bureaucratic methods are adopted to some extent by big concerns. But the critics of this phenomenon not only grotesquely exaggerate its scope, they blame the enterprise—as is the case with most of the faults they find in big business—for something that is the outcome of their own cherished policies of restricting and sabotaging the operation of business by government interference. Business management, also called profit management, is the method of conducting affairs for the best possible and cheapest provision of the consumers with all the commodities and services they are most urgently asking for. For the businessmen nothing counts but the approval of their actions by the buying public. Those who best succeed in satisfying the consumers earn profits. Those who fail in these endeavors suffer losses; if they do not learn the lesson and do not improve their conduct, they are forced to go out of business. Profit management means the full supremacy of the consumers. In this sense some economists called the market a democracy in which every penny gives a right to vote. Bureaucratic management is the management of affairs rendering services that on account of their peculiar character cannot be sold on the market to those benefited by them. The services a police department renders in curbing gangsterism are of the highest value for every citizen. But they cannot be sold piecemeal to the individuals in the way a railroad sells its services. As the "product" of the police activities has no market price, it is impossible to compare the effect of these activities with the costs expended in the way a business compares the costs expended in producing merchandise with the price at which it is sold on the market.

The services the shoe industry renders to the public could be considerably improved by increasing the amount of capital invested in this line of business. There would be more and cheaper shoes available for the consumers. But such an expansion of one industry could be brought about only by withholding or withdrawing capital and labor from other lines, e.g., from the production of shirts. The question is therefore whether or not the consumers approve of such an expansion of one industry and the restriction of some other industry necessarily induced by it. It is the consumers who by their comportment in buying shoes and shirts determine how much capital and labor should be dedicated to each of these industries. It is the profit motive that forces the entrepreneurs to employ to the best of their ability the material as well as the human factors of production according to the wishes of the consumers. The size of each industry and the quantity and quality of products it turns out are thus ultimately determined by the consumers. An entrepreneur who, defying the wishes of the consumers, would use—waste—capital and labor for the production of something for which the demand of the consumers is less urgent would be penalized by losses.

The service that the police department of a city renders to the public could certainly be improved by multiplying the funds devoted to it. But the question of whether or not the citizens consider the advantages to be expected from such an enlargement of the police department as a sufficient compensation for the additional expenditure with which it burdens them, cannot be decided in the way it is done in the case of commodities and services negotiated on the market. The accounts of the police department can only provide information about the expenses incurred. The results obtained by the money expended cannot be expressed in money equivalents. The citizens must directly determine the amount of services they want to get and the price they are prepared to pay for them. They discharge this task by electing councilmen whose duty it is to allocate the available funds to the various municipal services.

This is the fundamental difference between profit management and bureaucratic management. The activities of profit-seeking private business enterprise are subject to the most rigid control on the part of the buying public. Every firm, each of its subdivisions and branches, every employee is in all activities forced to comply with the wishes of the consumers. The ultimate standard in the conduct of business is provided by the accounts that confront expenditure with proceeds. An employee or a branch that absorbs more money than it contributes to the concern's gross yields is looked upon as a failure. All parts of a business concern whether large or small are committed to one principle only: make profits and avoid losses. That means: Serve the consumers.

But it is different with the administration of affairs the product of which has no price on the market. Here the confrontation of costs expended and prices paid by the public for the resulting services cannot serve as guidance. The constitutional institution that allocates a definite sum out of public revenue for their conduct must prescribe what quantity and what kind of services it wants to get from the department concerned. The budget and the instructions issued far the spending of the allocation provide the ultimate standard. In business there prevails the rule, provide what the consumers want to buy at prices exceeding the costs expended. In bureaucratic affairs the rule is to comply strictly with the instructions issued. There is no excuse for a man in business who does not satisfy the consumers. There is no excuse for a bureaucrat who defies the instructions issued by his superiors. The first thing a bureaucrat must try to find out when faced with a new problem is: What do the regulations say?

Bureaucratic management as such is not an evil. It is the only method available for the administration of the proper affairs of government. The public servants would become irresponsible despots if they were not obliged to behave in the conduct of the affairs entrusted them precisely in the way the authorities, the officeholders elected by the people, order them to behave. But bureaucratism turns into a nuisance if it invades the conduct of profit-seeking business and induces it to substitute for the business principle "serve the customer" the bureaucratic principle "comply with the regulations and instructions."

What makes big business adopt in some regards bureaucratic methods is not its size but the policies practiced today of government interference with business. As conditions are today it is more profitable for a concern to be on good personal terms with men in the various government agencies that are harassing business than to improve the services it renders to the consumers. The main problem for many enterprises is how to avoid as much as possible the animosity of officeholders. Men who for some reasons are not popular with the ruling party are considered unfit to manage the affairs of a company. Former employees of government agencies are hired by business, not on account of their abilities but on account of their connections. The boards of directors find it necessary to spend large sums out of the shareholders' property for purposes that have no relation to the company's business and do not yield anything for it but popularity with the administration and the party in power. In considering changes in production and marketing, the first question is often: "How will this move affect our public relations?" Big business is fully aware of the fact that the authorities have the power to harm it by proceeding further in the discriminatory methods of taxation and in many other regards. Big business is the main target in the undisguised war that government is waging against private enterprise.

In the last years a number of books—fiction and nonfiction—were published in which the bureaucracy of big companies has been taken to task. It escaped the notice of the public that the experience with which the authors of these books deal refers to those bureaus of the corporations that handle public relations and government affairs and not to the production and marketing of the goods they turn out. Apart from the effects of the union-enforced seniority rules, there is fortunately not yet too serious mischief done by bureaucratization in the conduct of the genuine operations of the plants.

People as Consumers vs. People as Voters

In their beginnings the attacks upon big business were prompted by the aspiration of some groups of artisans, shopkeepers, and small farmers for special privileges that would enable them to meet the competition of bigger outfits. In some countries this motive still plays a role. But with the further evolution economic affairs all people had to realize that there cannot be any question of a return to the conditions of the precapitalistic ages in which small units prevailed in almost all branches of production and distribution. Thus the meaning of the condemnation of bigness in business radically changed. It no longer suggests a return to medieval handicrafts. It is a plea for the establishment of all-round "planning" and "social control," i.e., government control of business. It is a plea for a step-by-step substitution of socialism of the *Zwangswirtschaft* (compulsory) type for the market economy. The long lists of the alleged crimes of big business compiled by the advocates of socialism cannot invalidate the fact that a nation is the more prosperous the more big business it has. The people of the United States enjoy the highest average standard of living because their country has

up to now hindered less the growth of enterprises into bigness than other countries.

The question to be decided is: Who should determine the
size of the enterprises, the consumers by their striving to buy
what suits them best or the politicians who know only how
to tax away and to spend?

It is true that the same people who in their capacity as consumers make the efficient suppliers' business grow into bigness, in their capacity as voters entrust the politicians with
the power to give free rein to their anti-business ventures. But
in considering this blatant inconsistency and contradiction
in the behavior of our contemporaries we must not forget the
fact that the ability of the average citizen to deal with the
issues of his own household and with those of economic policies is different. The housewife who buys one brand knows
what is best for herself and her family. She has learned from
experience and is fully competent to manage the affairs of
her household. But she and likewise her husband are certainly
less able to choose among various political and economic programs. Thus we see that the voters support policies that contra-
dict their own wishes and vital interests as manifested by their
behavior *qua* buyers and consumers. Here again the most
instructive example is provided by the American farm policies. The immense majority of the nation are in favor of cheap
prices for agricultural products. Nonetheless they have been,
for many decades, electing senators and congressmen committed to a policy of spending billions of the taxpayers' money
for measures to raise the prices of farm products far above
the height that would prevail on an unhampered market. This
policy of raising the prices of the vital necessities is so obviously nonsensical from whatever point of view you may judge
it that even cabinet secretaries of agriculture and members
of the President's Council of Economic Advisers condemned
it. But the voters are still voting for it.

Incidentally, we may add that most of the predominantly
industrial countries of Europe are also committed to a pol-

icy of artificially raising the prices of essential foodstuffs high above the level they would attain on a free market.

Thus we must not be too much astonished to realize that also in the matter of big business the average voter, deceived by ruthless propaganda, supports what hurts his own interests. There is only one means available to change this mentality. One has to try to instruct the public.

Notes

[1] Editor's note: *Die Meistersinger von Narnburg*, an opera by Richard Wagner (1813-1883) set in 16th-century Nuremburg. Hans Sachs is a kind and elderly *Meistersinger* (master singer) and cobbler whose shop is seen in several scenes. He enables a young knight to become a Meistersinger and win the hand of his ladylove.

[2] Editor's note: Prince Alois von Liechtenstein (1846-1920), a leader of the Austrian Christian Socialist Party and a social reformer. K. Freiherr [Baron] von Vogelsang, a convert to Catholicism and a theoretician of the Christian Socialists. Pierre Poujade, a French politician, responded to the dissatisfaction of farmers and small merchants with tax and economic policy, founding a short-lived movement, the Union de Défense des Commerçants et Artisans (UCDA), which in January 1956 won 52 seats in the National Assembly, but won none in 1962.

[3] V. I. Lenin, *State and Revolution* (New York: International Publishers, 1932), 43f.